MAKING
Wild
WINES &
MEADS

MAKING

Wild

WINES &

MEADS

125 Unusual Recipes Using Herbs, Fruits, Flowers & More

PATTIE VARGAS & RICH GULLING

Storey Publishing

The mission of Storey Publishing is to serve our customers by publishing practical information that encourages personal independence in harmony with the environment.

Edited by Brad Ring and Dan Callahan
Cover and interior design by Betty Kodela
Production assistance by Susan Bernier and Kelley Nesbit
Line drawings by Elayne Sears
Indexed by Peggy Holloway

Printed in the United States by Versa Press

20 19 18 17 16

Library of Congress Cataloging-in-Publication Data

Vargas, Pattie, 1941–
    Making wild wines & meads: 125 unusual recipes using herbs, fruits, flowers & more /
    Pattie Vargas & Rich Gulling.
        p. cm.
    Includes index.
    ISBN 978-1-58017-182-3 (paperback: alk. paper)
    1. Wine and winemaking Amateurs' manuals. 2. Mead Amateurs' manuals. I. Gulling,
    Rich, 1961– . II. Title. III. Title: Making wild wines and meads. IV. Title: Wild wines
    & meads. V. Title: Wild wines and meads.
TP548.2.V37 1999
641.8'72—DC21   99-23137
                                                                                       CIP
                                                                                       Rev.

For Gilbert and Carol Bohlman,

who, like fine wines,

only get better with age.

Contents

Chapter One

WINEMAKING MADE EASY

A few purists still think that the only good wine is a grape wine. *Making Wild Wines & Meads* is a book that may change their minds. Making wines and meads from fruits, vegetables, flowers, grains, honey, and herbs is an age-honored hobby whose time has come again. Now, making wonderful homemade wines from these natural and unusual ingredients has never been easier.

THE BASICS

If you are just getting your feet wet as a winemaker, here are a few basics. Finished wines contain from 7 to 14 percent alcohol (by volume) created by fermentation. For a solution to ferment, only three components are necessary — sugar, yeast, and nutrients. The rest of the ingredients in most recipes provide the flavors or improve the character and keeping quality of the wine. Here's how the process works: Yeast is a fungus with a sweet tooth. Feed it sugars and nutrients in solution, and the reward is alcohol and carbon dioxide — the by-products of the yeast's growth. The yeast continues to grow and multiply as long as it feels at home.

Yeasts generally have a few working rules that are strictly enforced. Violate the rules and they go on strike. Too little sugar, too much alcohol, too high or too low a temperature, too few nutrients — any of these will stop fermentation. Yeast does not like competition for the available nutrients and sugars, either. Let in bacteria, and there goes the neighborhood! As bacteria multiply, they create their own by-products. Some result in spoilage; one bacteria called *acetobacter* turns wine into vinegar. Most of the equipment and supplies you'll need to make wine help keep the ideal environment for yeast, so it will grow and produce wine. That means keeping out the bacteria and, in the later stages of fermentation, the oxygen, so the yeast can produce alcohol most efficiently.

WINEMAKING EQUIPMENT

Winemaking equipment generally falls into two categories: the "essential" and the "nice to have." Essential equipment includes those things that are needed at each part of the process. You will probably have some of the essential equipment in your kitchen already, and the rest you should be able to purchase rather inexpensively from a home winemaking supply store or mail-order catalog.

Essential Winemaking Equipment

If you are just beginning, the list on page 3 will provide you with the bare-bones equipment necessary to make your first batch of wild wine. Here are a few pointers:

Large Soup Kettle. This will be used for a number of purposes. The most important use is to heat those components of your wild wines that need cooking to release the flavors. *Do not* use iron or chipped enamel pots, or brass or copper kettles. Because wines and major wine ingredients are essentially acid, they can react with metals to form metal salts, some of which are toxic. In addition to the possible health hazard, these metals may react with fruit acids to make your wines hazy. Similarly, these same components may discolor aluminum kettles. For all these reasons, stay away from aluminum, copper, and brass pots when making wines. Stainless steel, glass, and unchipped enamel pots are your best choices.

- Large 3-gallon (11.4 L) soup kettle or Dutch oven, glass or stainless steel

- 5-gallon (19 L) primary fermentation bin or earthenware crock

- Assorted measuring cups and measuring spoons

- Long-handled wooden or plastic spoons, for stirring

- Plastic tubing, for siphoning

- Large plastic funnel

- Large strainer

- Several 1-gallon (3.8 L) jugs with handles, or collapsible plastic vessels, for secondary fermentation

- Several fermentation locks (also called airlocks)

- Wine bottles

- New corks to fit the wine bottles

- Notebook for keeping records

Basic winemaking equipment

Primary Fermentation Bin. The primary fermentation bin is usually made of white polypropylene — a hard, smooth plastic that is relatively inexpensive, easy to clean and sterilize, and without dyes that might impart unwanted flavors. Alternative containers are earthenware crocks; large, white plastic wastebaskets; and buckets. If you use old crocks, make sure that they are free of cracks and that they have not been treated with a glaze containing lead, which could cause lead to leach into your wine. Most crocks made in the United States in modern times are free from harmful metals in their glazes, but some crocks that come from Mexico or the Middle East may still have a lead glaze. Some historians believe that lead-poisoned wine, contaminated from storage containers, contributed to the downfall of the Roman Empire, because lead poisoning causes a decline in mental acuity. If you're not sure where the crock came from, don't use it.

Finally, although plastics are generally inert materials that do not react with wine, we try to stay away from colored plastic vessels because we are not sure whether dyes will affect the quality or flavors of wines. White and clear plastic containers are easy to clean and sterilize, and psychologically, they seem to feel cleaner.

Measuring Cups, Measuring Spoons, Stirrers, Funnels, and Strainers. These may be found in most kitchens. If you are buying them especially for winemaking, make sure that they are large and made of glass, metal, or plastic so they can be sterilized easily .

Plastic Tubing. We've always used clear plastic aquarium tubing for siphoning (also called *racking*) wine from one container to another. It's inexpensive, easy to clean, and free of dyes that might alter the flavor of the wine. Winemaking suppliers also carry a wide range of inexpensive tubing for racking.

Secondary Fermentation Bins. Several 1-gallon (3.8 L) jugs with handles or collapsible plastic fermentation vessels will be needed to hold your young wine during its secondary fermentation, when the fermentation slows down. Both glass and plastic bins must be able to be fitted with fermentation locks to keep out air. Glass and clear plastic are relatively inexpensive and easily cleaned. We use the collapsible fermentation vessels because they are also lightweight and portable.

Collapsible plastic fermentation bin

Used for secondary fermentation, the plastic bin is inexpensive and easy to clean.

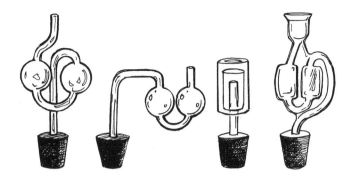

Fermentation locks

Even though they have vastly different shapes, each of these locks keeps the air out of the fermentation vessel.

Fermentation Locks. These simple plastic devices keep air out of your fermentation vessel during the critical second fermentation, when the necessary alcohol is created to give your wine good keeping qualities. They come in several configurations (see illustration) and are available wherever winemaking supplies are sold. We've tried several, and all of them seem to work equally well. All models work by holding a small amount of water to act as a barrier between outside air and the inside of your fermenter. They are also designed to allow any excess carbon dioxide created by the fermenting wine to escape the fermenter by venting through the water barrier.

Wine Bottles. Take special care with your wine bottles when you store the wines. Wine bottles aren't really expensive if you consider that you can use them again and again, as long as you keep them clean and sterilize them before each reuse. In this age of recycling, you can probably find quite a few friends who will save wine bottles for you as well. We almost always reuse the bottles from wines that we make or buy.

Wine bottles come in a variety of shapes — traditionally related to the region where the grape variety was grown or the kind of wine the bottle held, such as Burgundy, claret, Rhine wine, or champagne. The amount of wine a bottle holds is fairly standard. Most winemakers — and wine buyers, for that matter — assume that the standard bottle, holding approximately 25 ounces (750 ml), is what is meant by a "bottle" of wine. True, some wines are sold in half-gallon (1.9 L) containers, but these wines are usually called jug wines.

Bottle shapes

Left to right: bottles of Rhine wine, claret, Burgundy, and champagne.

Q&A CAN YOU USE LARGER JUGS TO BOTTLE WINES?

Any wine that is bottled in ½-gallon (1.9 L) or 1-gallon (3.8 L) containers — usually jugs with single or double handles — is properly called a jug wine. Because it is more commercially profitable to bottle fine vintage wines in the traditional 25-ounce (750 ml) wine bottle, the term "jug wine" has come to connote a cheaper or inferior wine. In some cases, that's an unfair designation, as there are a number of perfectly acceptable jug wines. When you bottle and cork your own wild wines, the designation becomes academic. If you entertain frequently and would normally consume more than one 25-ounce bottle of wine in the course of an evening, by all means bottle your wine in jugs. Just remember that wines are more prone to oxidize, or turn, once they have been opened, so bottle your wines in quantities that are likely to be consumed in a single seating.

New Corks. We avoid reusing corks. Used corks break easily; they may have gotten fat with absorbed liquids, which makes them difficult to insert into the bottles; and they may not fit properly. New corks are cheap and readily available. We use new, sterilized corks for bottling our wine. Some winemakers use caps to seal their wine bottles, but we don't recommend that practice. Traditionally, fine wines are corked and stored in a rack that keeps the bottles on their sides with the necks slightly lower than the bottoms. That position keeps the corks moistened with wine so they swell and form a tight seal. Screw-on caps may allow some air leakage, which will cause your wine to oxidize. Caps applied with a bottle capper just seem more appropriate for beer or soda pop than for wine. New corks cost only a few cents each and are well worth the investment.

Notebook. The whole winemaking process covers a lot of time. To be sure to remember when you are supposed to accomplish all the steps in the process, keep track with a pencil and your trusty notebook. But don't stop with recording dates. Keep notes. You may want to make a particular wine again, and your notes will let you know what to expect. You may have made adjustments along the way to create a superb wine. How can you duplicate it if you don't remember what you did?

When you make an adjustment in ingredients, for example, or if you have a problem, write it down. Keeping records may not be the most entertaining part of making wine, but you'll be glad you kept notes when the original recipe tastes so good that you just can't wait to make it again.

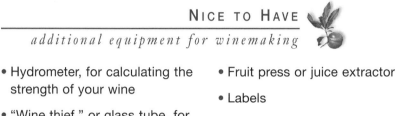
Additional Equipment

Hydrometer. You can make wine without having a hydrometer, but you'll have better, more consistent results if you learn how to use one. It seems a bit complicated at first, but it's really not difficult. With a hydrometer, you can:

- determine how much natural sugar is in your fruit juice;
- figure out how much sugar you will need in order to get a wine of the specific strength that you want;
- check how your fermentation is progressing;
- calculate the strength of a finished wine.

If you know, for example, how much natural sugar is in your fruit juice, you'll have a better idea of how much sugar or honey you must add to make a wine or a mead with sufficient alcohol so it tastes good and has good keeping quality. If you have a wine that has stopped fermenting, use your hydrometer to measure how much sugar is in the early stages of your wine (also called must.) Then you'll know whether the fermentation stopped because all the sugar was digested by the yeast, or if it is just stuck and in need of help. If you have calculated the amount of sugar needed to produce a certain strength of wine, you will have more control over how sweet or dry the finished wine will taste.

Hydrometers are instruments used for scientific measurement. In recent years, hydrometers specifically for winemaking have become available. They also indicate when it is safe to bottle a wine. The hydrometer works on a simple principle. The denser a liquid, the greater its gravity or weight and the easier it will be for an object to float in it. Water, for example, has a gravity of 1.000 — a number that scientists assigned to it so they would have a standard to measure against. If you add sugar to the water, it becomes denser. Then its specific gravity, or its gravity compared to water, will be a number higher than 1 — or 1 plus a decimal, such as 1.160. Because the number before the decimal is always 1 on the winemaker's hydrometer, it is usually omitted, and we say that the juice, must, or wine has a specific gravity of 160.

A hydrometer looks something like a thermometer with a weighted, bulbous end. The weighted end makes it float upright in a liquid, and to read it, you look at the printed scale at the exact point where the surface of the liquid cuts across the scale. The thinner the liquid, the more the hydrometer will sink; the thicker (or more dense and therefore sweeter) the liquid, the higher the hydrometer will float. For that reason, the scale has the lowest figures at the top and the highest at the bottom. If you put the hydrometer in a liquid that has less gravity than water, such as alcohol, it will sink even lower, and the specific gravity will be less than 1.000. A really dry wine could have a specific gravity of 995, for example.

The hydrometer comes with a small, tubular jar that you fill with the liquid to be measured. You put the hydrometer into the liquid, spin it around a couple of times to get rid of the air bubbles, then take your reading. Hydrometers are designed to be read at a specific temperature (59°F [15°C]), and the instructions that accompany it will have a chart for correcting the reading at different temperatures.

READING A HYDROMETER

When you look at the hydrometer floating in the glass tube filled with wine, must, or fruit juice, you'll notice that the liquid tends to "crawl" up the sides of the tube a bit, so the surface of the liquid is a bit like a very shallow U. Be sure to take your reading at the bottom of the liquid, not at the edge where it clings to the surface of the tube. (See illustration on page 9.)

Hydrometers designed specifically for wine-making come with charts that show you how much alcohol a specific amount of sugar will produce if the wine ferments completely so that all the sugar is used up. There are also instructions on how to calculate the amount of sugar to add to reach a specific strength (or, if the wine would be sweeter than you'd like at completion, how much to dilute it). Generally speaking, a really dry wine needs to start at a specific gravity of about 1.085, a medium or semisweet wine at 1.100, and a very sweet wine at about 1.125. For a dry wine, that usually works out to about 2½ pounds (1.1 kg) of sugar to 1 gallon (3.8 L) of liquid. If you use that rule of thumb to start, but want a sweeter wine, add a little simple syrup to the wine that's stopped fermenting, taste it, and refit the airlock.

Wine Thief. The easiest way to taste and adjust your fermenting batch of wine is by using a "wine thief," a device that looks like a glass drinking straw. Simply dip one end of the sterilized wine thief into the must or wine, put a thumb or finger over the other end, and lift the thief out of the wine. You can then drop a small amount on your tongue to taste-test, or you can fill up the hydrometer measuring tube.

Wine Corker. Another nice piece of equipment to have is a bottle corker. If you are making only small quantities of wine, push the corks into the bottles partway; wait a few days to make sure that the fermentation is finished so you won't have any cork popping, and then use a mallet and several thicknesses of folded cardboard to pound the corks completely into the bottles. For large quantities, however, this process is tedious. A bottle corker is a device that looks a little like an old-fashioned pump, with a handle and a plunger that forces the cork into a bottle.

Wine Filter. Wild wines and meads are sometimes quite difficult to clear. Substances such as pectin, starch, and protein can make your wines cloudy, and although those substances are not harmful, they do affect the appearance of your wine. Usually, given enough time, most wines will clear themselves. But if you've been patient and the wine simply will not clear, use a wine filter. Filtering may remove some flavors or aromas from the wine as well as the cloudiness, so use it as a last resort — but filtering is still better than throwing the wine away.

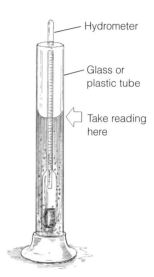

Hydrometer

Glass or plastic tube

Take reading here

Hydrometer reading
The liquid may climb up the sides of the tube slightly, assuming a cupped shape. Take your reading at the curved liquid's lowest point.

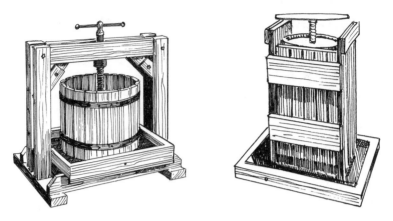

Fruit presses

Large and small fruit presses are available, but a small one meets the needs of most home winemakers.

Fruit Press. Particularly with wild wines, a fruit press or juice extractor comes in handy. Either will give you the maximum amount of juice with the least amount of work. Many different kinds are available from winemaking equipment supply houses, gardening catalogs, and home appliance departments.

Labels. Labels, carefully designed just for your wild wines, can be the finishing touch to a fine winemaking experience. Try to use a water-soluble glue to apply them, or you'll have trouble removing the labels when you want to reuse the bottles. Pressure-sensitive labels (found in any office supply store) also work well and are easily removed. Besides making your end product look more official, labels also serve as a valuable way to keep track of inventory and aging. Remember to note on the label the year and month of bottling as well as the type of wine; this will help you keep your records accurate.

Wine Thermometer and Heating Pad. Because the yeasts in your wine are likely to sulk if the temperatures are too hot or too cold, a wine thermometer — and perhaps a heating pad made especially for winemakers — is nice to have. If you make your wine in the living area of your home, the temperature that makes you comfortable (about 60 to 70°F [15 to 20°C]) will also satisfy your wine yeasts. Depending on the time of year, the location of your fermenting wine, and your own comfort, you may need to adjust the temperature, however. Moving your wine to a cooler location in the summer, or using a heating pad if you ferment in an unheated basement or porch, may make the wine yeast work more efficiently.

WINEMAKING SUPPLIES

Once you've assembled your equipment, you're ready to gather the supplies you'll need to make wine. The following list has the general supplies that most winemakers use regularly. Before you try a recipe in this book, read through the ingredient list to make sure that you have everything on hand.

STOCKING A WINEMAKER'S CUPBOARD

- Wine yeast

- Yeast nutrient

- Pectic enzyme

- Campden tablets or powder

- Flavoring component (usually juices, herbs, spices, honey, vegetables, or flowers)

- Sugar component (usually sucrose or honey; occasionally brown sugar)

- Acid blend (or citrus juices, in wild wines)

- Tannin (optional)

Wine Yeast

Yeast is made up of single-celled plants that grow in sugary solutions. As they grow, yeasts produce alcohol and carbon dioxide in about equal parts. Yeast cells accomplish this conversion of sugar to alcohol by producing enzymes that "digest" the sugars. Eventually, the yeast produces enough alcohol to kill the yeast cells themselves, and the dead yeast cells fall to the bottom of the wine-making vessel as *lees*, or sediment. Because different kinds of yeast cells have different tolerances for the amount of alcohol that will ultimately kill them, the kind of yeast you use helps determine the alcohol content of your wine.

Yeasts need certain conditions to reproduce favorably — warmth, oxygen, sugar, nitrogenous matter, vitamins, and acid. But because yeast is so important to the winemaking process, suppliers actually grow the most genetically efficient strains for use by winemakers. That is one of the reasons, in addition to taste and speed, that we prefer purchasing good-quality wine yeasts for our winemaking. It's a little like purchasing hybrid seed for your garden to guarantee healthier, better-adapted plants.

Q A IS THERE A "NO-YEAST" RECIPE FOR WINE?

Some winemakers make wine with nothing but grapes, but only because grapes already have yeast on their skins, and some of this yeast gets the fermentation process going. In most cases, though, the country wines in this book are made without grapes and must have yeast to ferment. Even when a recipe has grapes or raisins, the fruit may not have the best yeast for the job, so don't try to save a few cents on yeast; in the long run, you'll end up wasting the other ingredients in your wine if it doesn't ferment properly.

A lot of old-time winemakers used bread yeasts to make their wines because that was what was available, and you can make a number of acceptable wines by that method. The bread yeasts found in most supermarkets are from the same family as wine yeasts, but they are a different variety. The differences can be as pronounced as those between your cousin Mary and your uncle John. If you experiment with both kinds of yeasts, you will notice three major differences. First, most wine yeasts don't bubble as much or as energetically in the first fermentation as do bread yeasts. The more subdued bubbling means that fewer fragrance elements are carried off with the carbon dioxide, so a wine made with a wine yeast tends to have a better bouquet. Second, wine yeasts tend to leave firmer sediment at the bottom of the fermentation vessels than do bread yeasts. That makes racking easier because you will be less likely to stir up sediment when you siphon off the wine. Last, the taste will be better because wine yeasts come in a number of varieties for different kinds of wines. That lets you pick a yeast that suits the kind of wine you are making — a port yeast for a deep red wine, for example.

Choosing the Right Wine Yeast Strain. Wine yeasts come originally from the skins of grapes, and each variety of grape has a slightly different variety of yeast. These yeasts are collected and cultured, then sold by the packet. A good rule of thumb in choosing wine yeasts is to look at the kind of grape wine that each yeast makes. You'll find yeast for port, sherry, Tokay, Madeira, Malaga, Sauternes, and Burgundy, among others. For making a dark red wine — from elderberries or blackberries, for example — choose a yeast used to make a dark red grape wine such as port or Burgundy. We use champagne yeast for honey wines because we like the taste. Wine yeasts are relatively inexpensive and you can extend what you buy by making your own yeast starter cultures, so we suggest that you experiment — it's part of the fun of making your own wines.

Home winemakers were once fairly limited in the kinds of yeasts they could buy. Today there are dozens. A few of the better ones and some suggestions for their use are listed in the following table.

MAKING THE MOST OF YEASTS		
KIND OF YEAST	QUALITIES OF YEAST	USES OF YEAST
ASSMANSHAUSEN	Ferments slowly; somewhat spicy; sometimes needs added tannin ingredient	Red wines
BEAUJOLAIS	Strong fermentation; fruity taste	Red wines with fruity flavors; especially nice for berries
CALIFORNIA CHAMPAGNE, UCD 505	Settles out easily, in clumps; makes racking easier	Honey wines; white wines made from aromatic fruits
CHANSON	Medium fermentation rate; produces fewer sulfites than most; needs sufficient nutrients or it sticks; settles out well for easy racking; refined flavors	Nice for fruit wines, especially apples
EPERNAY 2	Ferments slowly; aromatic; foamy; good bouquet; prefers cooler temperatures	Fruit wines, especially those that will be white, such as peach, pear, apricot, and plum
FERMIVIN	Fast fermentation; watch out for bubbling over; goes readily to dryness; great to fix stuck fermentations; clean taste	Recommended for red wines
MONTRACHET	Produces more sulfites than some; ferments fast and hot; occasionally sticks	Red wines with strong, full flavors
PASTEUR CHAMPAGNE	Good all-purpose yeast; goes to dryness easily; ferments quickly; nice clean flavor	White wines; honey wines; melomels with peaches, pears, plums, or apricots
PASTEUR RED	Ferments fast, strong	Best for full-bodied red wines; use with berries
PASTEUR WHITE	Produces lots of foam and goes to dryness; flavors are more acid than fruity; keep temperatures even	Nice for white wines with crisp flavor
PRISE DE MOUSSE	Slow, even fermentation; yeasty aroma; clean flavor	A good all-purpose yeast
STEINBERG	Needs cool temperatures; nice bouquet, complex and fruity	Good for German-style wines

Yeast Nutrient

Yeasts need certain organic compounds to grow and reproduce efficiently, just as do all plants and animals. Most of the time, wines made with fruit have these organic nutrients because the fruit provides them. But some wines, especially those made with honey, lack these compounds. If you fail to provide them in some way, the yeast will grow for a while and then quit. When yeast stops growing, the wine never reaches its full alcohol potential, and it becomes vulnerable to spoilage. As it is difficult to measure just how much of each nutrient is present in the must, we generally add yeast nutrient as a kind of insurance against "malnutrition." Even in those kinds of wine that have essential growth nutrients, fermentation is often faster and more efficient if yeast nutrients are added.

You can purchase a mix of yeast nutrients through winemaking suppliers. These nutrients are an inexpensive, quick, and easy way to provide what the yeasts need. You can also boost the necessary nutrients for good yeast growth by adding citrus juices to your batch. With the juices, you'll also gain the acid component that gives wines their character. (Any fruit pulp provides nutrients, but the citrus in most of our wild wine recipes affects the flavor of the wine the least. Citrus adds mostly acid instead of strong flavors.) A commercial yeast nutrient, however, is a kind of vitamin pill for your wine. If you've formulated your wines with juices to supply these nutrients, you may not need to add yeast nutrient at all, but why take the chance?

WHAT'S IN THERE?

Commercial yeast nutrients contain any of the following: ammonium sulfate, magnesium sulfate, potassium phosphate, diammonium phosphate, ammonium chloride, and thiamine.

Pectic Enzyme

Particularly with honey wines and meads, but also with wines made from certain high-pectin fruits such as underripe apples, clarity is a problem even after diligent racking. The cloudiness probably results from too much pectin — the substance that turns fruit juice into jelly. Although murky wine won't hurt you, it's not pretty, especially if it's a white or golden wine. Adding pectic enzyme to these wines when you make them usually solves the problem; the enzyme digests the pectin that keeps the wine from clearing.

Generally speaking, enzymes are naturally occurring proteins that aid plants and animals in breaking down complex substances, such as sugars and starches, into simpler forms. Pectic enzyme helps to break down pectin, a complex molecule found in many fruits, into simple sugars. When you add pectic enzyme to a wine recipe, you are making sure that any pectin present in the fruits you have used is turned into sugars, which fermentation will turn into alcohol and carbon dioxide. Not only will you have a more complete fermentation, but you will also have a clearer, more brilliant wine.

Campden Tablets or Powder

The easiest way to keep your wine free of wild yeasts and bacteria is to use a Campden tablet. An individual Campden tablet contains about 7 grains of potassium metabisulfate, which will eliminate wild yeasts and bacteria from winemaking equipment by releasing sulfur dioxide gas when dissolved in water. Use one tablet per gallon (3.8 L). You can also immerse fermentation locks and tubing in the solution just before you use them.

When you dissolve a tablet in any slightly acid solution, such as wine must, it releases approximately 4 grains of sulfur dioxide. At that concentration, one tablet in a gallon (3.8 L) of wine results in about 60 parts per million of sulfur dioxide. It is an effective sterilizing agent at that concentration because it stops the growth of spoilage organisms but does not affect the taste of the wine except to make it marginally more acid — which is almost always a plus. Your must will remain sterile for just 24 hours. Then you can add a prepared yeast culture, and your wine will be bubbling in no time. Even if they choose not to use Campden tablets, some winemakers let ingredients sit for 24 hours, well covered, before adding yeast to the must so that flavors permeate the juices. Although they are always optional, a Campden tablet works with any recipe in this book.

Flavoring Component

For our wild wine and mead recipes, we concentrate on non-grape ingredients to create unusual drinks, often using locally produced ingredients. These include juices, herbs, spices, honey, vegetables, nuts, and even flowers. If you are thinking about adding some local ingredients not mentioned in our recipes, please beware that some herbs and flowers are poisonous. The area of greatest concern is probably flowers. Because most people use flowers only for decoration, written information about them does not usually say whether they are toxic in food or beverages. Here are some plants to avoid ingesting: acacia, alder, azalea, belladonna, black nightshade, bluebell, buttercup, carnation, chrysanthemum, columbine, Christmas rose (hellebore), clematis, cotoneaster, crocus, cyclamen, daffodil, dahlia, delphinium, foxglove, geranium, hemlock, henbane, holly, honeysuckle berries, laurel, lilac, lily of the valley, lobelia, lupine, marsh marigold, meadow rue, mistletoe, monkshood, oleander, peony, poppy, rhododendron, rhubarb leaves, and sweet pea. There are undoubtedly others, so here is a good rule of thumb: If you're not sure, don't use it. In addition to these plants, avoid fungi of any kind, even mushrooms, and be sure to check an herb encyclopedia before you make herbal wines; the properties of herbs are usually well documented.

TIPS FOR USING CITRUS PEELS TO FLAVOR WINE

Look carefully at citrus fruit when you peel it, and you will notice that an orange, for example, has a thin, orange rind, a white fibrous substance (the inner rind), and the pulp of the fruit, in that order. If you sample the white substance beneath the orange rind, you will find a rather bland-tasting part of the citrus. But if that same bland substance is added to wine must and allowed to sit for several days or weeks as the fermentation continues, a bitter component is released into your wine. If you peel the fruit before you begin making wine, this white inner rind adheres to the essential-oil–rich outer rind, and it is very difficult to separate the two. The best method for removing the citrus zest, or outer rind, is with a vegetable peeler or zester. A fine grater also works well if you don't grate too deeply. Then remove the white inner rind as you would if the orange part were still attached, and discard it. That should prevent unwanted bitterness in your wine.

Sugar Component

Almost all of the recipes in this book call for refined sugar, except for the honey-based wines and meads. We have never found any discernible difference among most sugars in terms of taste, fermentability, or keeping quality. Because refined sugar is abundant and inexpensive, we think it is the best option for winemakers. One or two recipes call for brown sugar — mostly for the flavor, appropriate to those particular wines.

Acid Blend

The ideal wine has an acid content that is in balance with the tannins and sweeteners of the wine. Some fruits that make an otherwise delicious wine are lacking in sufficient acid for good taste. When the acid component in the must is too low, fermentation may be poor and the wine can develop a medicinal taste.

Most acid blends contain 1 part citric acid, 2 parts malic acid, and 3 parts tartaric acid. All of these are natural acids, found in various fruits. Fruits rich in citric acid include oranges, lemons, currants, strawberries, raspberries, and tangerines. Because citric acid also adds a nice fruitiness and brilliance to the wine, some winemakers routinely use citrus juice as their only acid component. Those who opt for an acid blend, including malic acid and tartaric acid, say that these two acids help to speed fermentation and improve the vinous character of the wine. Malic acid is found naturally in apples, apricots, blackberries, dark cherries, plums, gooseberries, nectarines, and rhubarb. Tartaric acid usually comes from grapes.

The acid of a particular fruit or flower can be measured through a process called titration, and some winemaking suppliers sell kits for that purpose; but we think the process is complicated and probably not worth the effort for those who make wines at home. Some winemakers use litmus paper and compare the color of the strip to a prepared chart. But because there are other things in wine besides acid that affect the measurement, the litmus test seems no more accurate than just tasting the wine and adjusting accordingly. As you become experienced at winemaking and tasting, you will become surprisingly adept at judging whether you need to add acid. In the meantime, rely on the supplier's directions in relation to the amount of acid in your ingredients.

Generally speaking, flowers and vegetables have little acid of their own, and wines made from these ingredients need about 2 teaspoons (10 g) of acid added per gallon (3.8 L). To help you estimate

ACID LEVELS		
LOW ACID	MEDIUM ACID	HIGH ACID
Beets	Apples	Blackberries
Dates	Apricots	Currants
Dried fruits	Cherries	Gooseberries
Elderberries	Grapes	Loganberries
Figs	Juice concentrates	Quinces
Flowers	Nectarines	Raspberries
Herbs	Oranges	Rhubarb
Pears	Peaches	Strawberries
Rose petals	Plums	
	Tangerines	

how acid your ingredients are, look at which ingredients fall into the low-, medium-, and high-acid levels on the chart above.

Tannin

Another ingredient that you will find listed in some of our recipes is tannin, or grape tannin. A component of the skins and stems of some fruits — especially red fruits like grapes, plums, apples, and elderberries — tannins do a number of nice things to your wines. First of all, they give wine a certain zip by creating a hint of dryness in the mouth when you sip the wine. Wines that have no tannins are generally dull and flat. But if you've ever tasted wine that draws your mouth into a pucker — usually a dark red wine — you'll know that too much tannin can make a wine bitter and astringent-tasting as well. As with most wine elements, the trick is to balance the tannins with the other ingredients. In those recipes in which we added tannin, the finished wine seemed a bit characterless without it. If you find that your wine lacks character or zest, you can add tannin, or 1 tablespoon (15 ml) of strong tea to 1 gallon (3.8 L) of wine, and you'll be pleased with the improvement. Equally important, tannins enhance a wine's keeping qualities.

In the wild wine recipes that are likely to be short on tannins — wines made from flowers, herbs, grains, or vegetables — we add them. This need for tannins is one of the reasons that so many wild wine recipes call for raisins. But there are other ways to add tannins to your wines. Some strong tea or even a few oak leaves added to the must will give added zest to recipes that you have found a bit dull. Or you can add commercial tannins, available from winemaking suppliers.

THE WINEMAKING PROCESS

The chart below outlines the seven basic steps in the winemaking process. It also estimates the time it will take you to complete each step. For a more detailed description of the winemaking process, see pages 20 to 37.

THE WINEMAKING PROCESS	
STEPS IN THE PROCESS	TIME NEEDED FOR COMPLETION
Step 1: Sterilize all winemaking equipment.	About ½ hour, depending on method
Step 2: Assemble the necessary ingredients. Wash all fruits, choosing only those that are ripe and unblemished; make up the must.	½ to 1½ hours
Step 3: Add yeast. Put the must into a fermentation container, tightly covered, and let stand for about 10 days, stirring once or twice daily; cover again (even 1 fruit fly in the must can introduce bacteria that will turn your wine to vinegar).	10 days
Step 4: Strain out the solids from your wine or rack it into a fermentation jar, bottle, or collapsible container to which you can affix a fermentation lock. Make sure all equipment is sterile. Allow the wine to ferment in the airlocked container until it is clear.	Several weeks
Step 5: When the wine has cleared, rack it into a sterile container to which you can affix a fermentation lock. Repeat this step as needed, usually one to two months later; repeat again if necessary.	1 to 3 months
Step 6: Bottle the wine; stabilize if desired. Cellar the wine in a cool location, storing bottles on their sides to keep the corks moist and tight.	Best if used before 3 or 4 years have elapsed. Will keep indefinitely if corks remain tight and temperatures are cool and constant.
Step 7: Use a corkscrew to open your wine. Enjoy.	Allow red wines to breathe, opened, for about ½ hour before serving at room temperature; chill white wines and serve immediately.

Step One: Sterilize All Winemaking Equipment

About the only mistakes in winemaking that cannot be remedied by tasting, adjusting, or blending result from contamination — that is, having something in the wine that alters the final flavor or results in spoilage. Always use squeaky-clean equipment. Sterilize anything that comes into contact with your wine, because everything is likely to carry microorganisms.

Boiling and scalding everything used for winemaking is one way to sterilize equipment. Today, though, most winemakers rely on easier methods. If you prefer to use at-hand materials, add 2 or 3 tablespoons (30 to 45 ml) of unscented household chlorine bleach to your dishwasher and run through the complete cycle all the equipment that will fit. Then run it through the rinse cycle a second time to make sure not a trace of chlorine remains — you don't want your wines to taste like bleach. You can also add 2 tablespoons (30 ml) of unscented household bleach to a gallon (3.8 L) of water. Soak your equipment in this solution for at least 10 minutes, rinse with water, and use immediately.

Step Two: Collect Ingredients, Prepare Must

Winemaking, even in small quantities, is ingredient intensive. You'll find the process less expensive if you keep stable ingredients such as pectic enzyme or yeast nutrient on hand, and then make wine when the fruit or honey is in season — berry wines in late spring or early summer, for example, and apple wines in the fall.

Washing the Fruit. Old-time winemakers who made wine only from grapes were often reluctant to remove the "bloom," or naturally occurring yeast, from the grapes because it was essential to the fermentation process for those who had no yeasts to add to the must. But times and conditions have changed drastically since the early winemakers grew grapes without sprays and in air that was free of environmental pollutants. Now, yeasts are added to the must, and the only reason for not thoroughly washing fruits is gone. We suggest that you place in a colander whatever fruit you are going to use, and run cool water over it for several minutes before you begin winemaking. Washing fruit later in the process, after skins and pits have been removed, results in a loss of juices. Never use overripe or spoiling fruit.

Juicing the Fruit. There are almost as many ways to extract fruit juices as there are winemakers who want to do it. Some like to ferment their wines on the pulp of chopped or mashed fruit, introducing the yeast right away, and draining the juice off a week or 10 days later. If color and pulp are important to the recipe, they sometimes put the

Q&A

DOES IT MAKE ANY DIFFERENCE WHAT KIND OF WATER I USE FOR MAKING THE MUST?

Make sure your water comes from a pure source. We use tap water, but we bring it to a boil for a few minutes to remove any chlorine and to kill any possible bacteria. If your water is very hard, you may want to use distilled water in your winemaking because the minerals have been removed from it. Softened water usually has sodium ions, so we don't recommend it for winemaking. In addition, some winemakers think that softened water alters the taste of the wine.

---

solids into a jelly bag or wrap them in cheesecloth. Then they either squeeze out the juices or let gravity extract them by hanging the jelly bag over a crock or bucket. French, German, and Italian winemakers prefer pressing — but we don't like to think too hard about stomping grapes for wine. If you want to press your fruits, small fruit presses are available from winemaking equipment suppliers. More-modern wine-makers use juice extractors, which have the advantage of being good for juicing fruits and vegetables for other purposes as well.

Some wine recipes call for boiling the fruit or vegetables and then draining off the juice. Employ this method with care — don't over-cook, or you'll have trouble getting the wine to clear.

Finally, many winemakers simply chop or crush the fruit and pour boiling water over it to remove the juice and the flavor. This also kills most wild yeasts and bacteria. Many of our wild wine recipes suggest this method, but you can use whatever suits your situation.

Making the Must. Making the must is the basic process of com-bining the sugar and flavoring ingredients with water in the ferment-ing bin. Be aware after juicing your fruit that inadvertently including crushed seeds, stems, or parts of the fruit that you would not normally eat — grape pips, the white inner rind of citrus fruits, the green fringe around flower blossoms, and any unripe parts of fruits — can cause off-flavors and even spoilage of a batch.

Most of our recipes call for adding a Campden tablet and allow-ing the must to sit, well covered, for 24 hours before adding yeast. Sterilizing the must with a Campden tablet will usually prevent unwanted bacteria from growing or mold from forming on your ingredients. But if you don't want the additional sulfites that result from a tablet, or if you don't keep the must completely covered during the first fermentation, mold could grow on a cap made up of fruit particles and other solids if it is exposed to airborne molds. In most cases this mold is not harmful, and you don't have to discard the wine. Just be careful not to stir the moldy cap into the wine.

Hydrometer Reading. After preparing the must, but before you add the yeast, you can take a hydrometer reading to determine how much sugar is in your must. You'll need a reading of at least 1.085 or you'll have to add more sugar to your batch to provide the yeast with enough nutrients to create the proper level of alcohol. Readings above 1.125 are on the high side and tend to produce overly sweet or alcoholic-tasting wine. The lower the number, the drier the wine.

Step Three: Add Yeast for Primary Fermentation, Stir the Must

Yeast is the magic ingredient in winemaking. Without this living component, your other ingredients are little more than fruit punch. Understanding yeast and treating it with care is therefore a crucial part of making winning wines.

Preparing a Yeast Starter. Most old wine recipes use the same or similar methods of preparation — crushing fruit, adding sugar or honey, and adding yeast, either by spreading it on a slice of bread and floating it on top of the must or by sprinkling dry yeast into the must mixture. Once the yeast is in the must, it begins to grow, but sometimes it takes several days for it to multiply enough to start a vigorous first fermentation. You can speed up this process with a yeast starter. Aside from the satisfaction of being able to speed up *anything* in the winemaking process, we think a vigorous fermentation that begins immediately results in a fresher-tasting wine. We also use a yeast

STAYING ON SCHEDULE

We set up a calendar in our computers with prompts to notify us when each step should be taken in the process. We just program them in at the beginning and wait for the messages. If things take a little longer than we thought, we adjust. You can also use a spreadsheet program or your trusty pencil on a wall calendar or in a notebook for reminders.

starter because it reduces the possibility of having a stuck fermentation. You are certain that the yeast is already viable and actively growing in the starter culture when you add it to your wine.

Essentially, a yeast starter culture is made by inoculating a small quantity of fruit juice with wine yeast (and yeast nutrients) to encourage the yeast to multiply rapidly. When you add this starter culture to your wine, it is already filled with growing yeast cells; thus fermentation is more efficient. Making a starter culture is simple. Just add a package of wine yeast (5 to 7 g) and 1 teaspoon (5 g) of yeast nutrient to 1½ cups (360 ml) of tepid fruit juice in a small, sterilized container. Cover, shake vigorously, and let stand at room temperature for 1 to 3 hours, until it gets bubbly. Orange juice makes an all-purpose starter culture, because the orange flavor is mild enough that you can use it in any kind of wine without affecting the final flavor. However, you may substitute an equal amount of juice from the fruit you are using in your wine, if you prefer.

To increase the ingredients in a recipe to make more wine — say 5 gallons instead of 1 — you don't have to add more starter culture. The yeast in your wine is alive and growing, and it will continue to grow in the must until it has converted the sugar in the mixture to the maximum concentration of alcohol that a given yeast will tolerate.

Adding Yeast to the Must. Always be sure to let the wine ingredients cool before adding yeast; too much heat will kill wine yeasts. The must should be at room temperature — about 60 to 70°F (15 to 20°C). Pour the yeast into the must and stir with a sterilized spoon. If you use a yeast starter, the must should begin to bubble within 12 to 24 hours. With dry yeast, it may take a day or two for active fermentation to begin. After adding the yeast, cover the container tightly with a lid.

ADDING SUGAR IN STAGES

Too much sugar can overwhelm the yeast in the must, just as can too much alcohol. Then the fermentation has a difficult time getting started. When we have found that to be a problem with a particular wine, we specify in our recipes to add the sugar in stages. Some winemakers do that routinely, as a kind of insurance policy, and there is no harm in doing so. We think using a yeast starter culture is also insurance against slow start-ups — and it requires less record keeping than does adding sugar in stages.

Primary Fermentation: Stirring the Must. During the first, also called primary, fermentation, the yeast in the wine grows rapidly, using oxygen and producing alcohol and carbon dioxide. This phase of fermentation lasts about 10 days. To aid fermentation in this active period, it is important to stir the must once or twice daily with a sterilized spoon so the oxygen in the air mixes into your wine. If a cap of fruit forms at the top of the must, punch a hole in it, push it down, and stir. If this cap has mold growing on it, do not stir the mold into the wine; depending on the composition of the mold, it could give your wine unwanted flavors. After stirring quickly, re-cover the fermenter tightly. It is important always to re-cover the bin during this first fermentation so no fruit flies contaminate the mixture.

Once started, your wine will usually bubble along happily at 60 to 70°F (15 to 20°C). The only time it might be appropriate to add heat to the process is if you are making wine in a cold porch, garage, or outbuilding or in a very cool basement. In that case, a winemaker's heating pad under your fermenting wine will keep things perking along. But heating the must to higher temperatures than those supplied by a heating pad in hopes of speeding up the process is sure to backfire. Get it too warm and the yeast will stop growing or die. Then, if you hope to salvage your ingredients at all, you must start at the beginning, adding a yeast starter culture and waiting. Finally, a too energetic fermentation usually means that some of the aromatic parts of the wine — the parts that give it its bouquet — are bubbled off with the carbon dioxide. The result is a wine that has much less bouquet than if you had patiently fermented your wine at proper temperatures. If you happen to have a wine in a warm spot that is fermenting very energetically during its primary fermentation, just sniff. If you smell bouquet disappearing in the bubbles, you may want to move your wine to a cooler spot, even if the fermentation does take longer. Waiting is what really good winemakers do best.

Step Four: Strain Out Solids, Rack into Secondary Bin

A visiting friend once observed the container of fermenting wine on our kitchen countertop being readied for racking and said, "Ick! You're not going to drink *that*?" "Not until it's racked," we answered. Racking takes the "ick" out of wine.

Straining. When the primary fermentation has slowed, after about 10 days, strain out any remaining pieces of fruit, skins, and other large ingredients that remain in the must. It's best to use a plastic racking tube to transfer the must to a sterilized secondary fermentation bin with an airlock, rather than simply pouring the must through a strainer.

Winemakers say wine is stuck or the fermentation is stuck if the fermentation process stops before the optimum amount of sugar is converted to alcohol, so the wine ends up oversweet. If you taste the wine and it is too sweet, there are a couple of possibilities. You may have inadvertently added too much sugar and the wine reached its limit of alcohol tolerance before enough sugar had fermented out. If you measure with a hydrometer, the specific gravity is too high. Or maybe the temperature is too low or too high. Perhaps some organic nutrient is missing. If the wine "sticks" during the first fermentation, it may be lacking in oxygen. If the same thing happens during secondary fermentations, the carbon dioxide may have become too concentrated and caused the wine yeast to stop growing.

When the problem is with the temperature, you can usually restart the fermentation by moving the vessel to a warmer or cooler spot and adding a little starter culture. If you have simply added too much sugar, dilute the mixture with water or juice so that the alcohol content is reduced, and fermentation will resume. If you didn't add a yeast nutrient to your starter culture, try giving your wine a little vitamin lift: Either add some yeast nutrient to a small container of the wine and then add it back to the must, or add just the tip of a teaspoon of Epsom salts or 3 milligrams of vitamin B_1 (thiamine). If all these remedies fail, you'll probably need to solve the problem one step at a time. First, make ½ pint (240 ml) of starter culture. When it is actively fermenting, add an equal amount of the stuck wine. Wait until this mixture starts to ferment, and repeat the process until all of your stuck wine has been added and the whole batch is actively fermenting. Also check that your fermentation lock is not plugged, keeping the carbon dioxide trapped inside the fermentation vessel.

Using a traditional strainer to transfer the must is recommended only in the early stages of fermentation. For wines that are further along in the process, racking causes less contact with oxygen or possible contaminants than does straining by pouring. Also, those wines that are further along will be clearer with this method: Racking leaves behind not only the big pieces of fruit, but also all the tiny particles that make for cloudy wines — dead yeast cells, minute fruit bits, and so on. These will have sunk to the bottom of the container and will remain there when you rack. Finally, straining may seem easier if you haven't racked wines before, but racking is more efficient. Waiting for the wine to run through the tubing may take a little longer, but the quality of the wine will be better. Once you feel confident enough to make large quantities of wine, you'll find that it's nearly impossible to lift big containers and dump them through a strainer without a lot of splashing and sloshing.

Racking. The most time-consuming — and intimidating — step in the winemaking process is racking. Yes, it takes time, but it needn't be intimidating. Simply stated, racking is siphoning wine into a new container and leaving the lees, or residue, behind.

In addition to clear plastic tubing, you'll need a way to raise the container of wine to be racked above the container you're racking the wine into. An upended bucket on the countertop works well to raise the container you will be racking *from*. If you then put the container you'll be racking *to* into the sink, any spills go down the drain.

Insert the tubing or siphon into the wine in the higher container, making sure that you don't put the tube all the way to the bottom of the container (where it would pick up sediment). Suck on the free end of the tubing much as you would on a drinking straw. You'll get a taste of wine, and it will flow downward as long as you keep this end of the tube below the end in the container of wine that you are racking from. Quickly place the free end of the tube into the container in the sink, and the wine should continue to flow until you remove the tube or until enough wine is siphoned into the second container so that the end is no longer in the wine in the higher container. The most important caution for racking is to make sure that you don't insert the racking tube so deeply into the container that you inadvertently pick up

LABEL YOUR WINES

If you have more than one kind of wine going at once, buy a supply of sticky labels at a stationery or office supply store and label each fermentation vessel with the name of the wine and the date you'll perform each operation. That way you won't start racking the mulberry wine when you're supposed to be racking the raspberry melomel.

Racking

Place the lower container, into which you're racking the wine, in the sink to avoid the problem of messy spills.

the lees. The whole point of racking is to separate the clear wine from the sediment.

Secondary Fermentation. The secondary fermentation bin, whether glass or plastic, needs to be fitted with a sterilized fermentation lock (an airlock). After this container is airlocked, the yeast switches to a new type of growth. In this mode, more alcohol is produced, and the yeast tolerates the alcohol better when no oxygen is present. The fermentation will be much slower than in the primary phase, but carbon dioxide will build up and be released through the airlock on the bin. At this point, your wine should begin to clarify. It usually takes several weeks for the young wine to clear enough to rack once again.

BEAT THE HEAT

In summer, it may be tough to maintain the 60 to 70°F (15 to 20°C) optimum fermentation temperature. Some winemakers put their airlocked fermentation vessels into a tub of water in the coolest spot they can find. The evaporation that results will cool down the fermenting wine (fermentation generates some of its own heat).

Q_A WHAT HAPPENS IF MY WINES WON'T CLEAR?

Wines become cloudy for a number of reasons. First, if you disturb the sediment when you rack the wine, some of the suspended particles might mix back into the wine. If this happens, an additional racking several days later may be all it takes to clear the wine. Some overzealous home winemakers attempt to clear by filtering their wines through filter paper, such as a coffee filter, or an aquarium charcoal filter. We don't recommend this because in addition to sediment, the process often removes other components of the wine, such as its elusive bouquet, its subtle flavors, or its characteristic color. Filtering also exposes the wine to additional air, which can lead to oxidation and spoilage. If you must filter — and filtering is preferable to cloudy wine — use a wine filter, available from winemaking equipment suppliers. Most use pressure, often applied by pumping, to force the wine through a filtering medium. But wines that clear naturally, with careful racking, are always the best wines.

Even with careful racking, a wine may remain stubbornly murky, and in that case the culprit is probably pectin, starch, or protein. Most of our recipes call for pectic enzyme because it is easier to prevent pectin cloudiness than to cure it. Similarly, another enzyme, amylozyme, turns starch, which cannot be fermented, into sugar, which can. Treating your wine with this enzyme will clear it if starch is the problem. Protein cloudiness is treated by a process known as fining — using a substance such as bentonite to clear the wine. Fining usually requires an exact dosage based on the amount of protein in the wine, and for that reason it is not frequently used by amateur winemakers.

Our ancestors had an inexact but rather effective way of dealing with cloudy wine. They dried a broken eggshell in the oven for a few seconds and then dropped it into the wine. Many modern commercial wineries include albumen — egg whites — among their collection of fining agents. Some of that substance may remain on the eggshell, and the shell itself absorbs impurities (sometimes, unfortunately, including color). So if all else fails, by all means try the eggshell treatment.

Step Five: Clear and Rack, Clear and Rack, Final Adjustments

Good wine appeals to all the senses. Connoisseurs love the splash of the wine as it's poured into a wineglass, the bouquet of the wine as they hold it under their noses, the texture and taste of the wine as they sip it — even the aftertaste as they swallow the wine and, the mouth cleansed, exhale slowly through their noses. If a wine makes a bad visual first impression, however, a real wine lover may never taste it at all. Fine wines must be clear and sparkly.

Clearing the Wine. In several weeks, after your wine has cleared in the secondary fermentation bin, it's time to rack into another sterilized container (also fitted with an airlock). In another one to two months, when the wine has cleared again, rack into yet another fermentation container. With each racking, be careful not to disturb or transfer the sediment. The primary goal here is to achieve a clear, clean-tasting wine. These steps can be repeated as many times as necessary in order to end up with the clearest wine possible.

USE YOUR MARBLES

Keep a supply of glass marbles on hand and add them to the air-locked fermentation vessels to keep the containers as full as possible, thus avoiding too much contact with air. This works great for partially filled airlocked jugs. If you do try this trick, make sure the marbles have been sterilized.

Adjusting Sweetness. A wine continues to ferment and turn sugar into alcohol and carbon dioxide until it reaches the point at which the alcohol is concentrated enough to prevent the yeast from growing further — usually about 14 percent alcohol (by volume). At this point, whatever sugar that has not been converted to alcohol and carbon dioxide remains to sweeten the wine. If you taste the wine when it has stopped fermenting and it is too dry, it is likely that the fermentation process has used up the sugars present and stopped when this source of energy ran out. You can add more sugar now either by dissolving some in a little of the wine and returning the mixture to the fermentation vessel, or by making a simple syrup — made by dissolving sugar in boiling water and then cooling it — and pouring it into the wine. If the wine begins to ferment again, it has not reached its highest concentration of alcohol, and it will use up some of the extra sugar to resume the fermentation process. By adding sugar a little at a time, monitoring the fermentation process, and sampling at intervals, you should be able to adjust the sweetness of the wine to suit your taste.

Keep a record of how much sugar you add, and don't add too much at a time. When you have the perfect combination, adjust the recipe accordingly for the next batch. If you use a hydrometer, record the reading at each stage of the process, and adjust according to the readings you like. A hydrometer allows you to adjust at the beginning of the fermentation process, and you may find that your wines turn out just as you like them without the repeated tasting and adding of sugar. However, we like to taste regardless: It's one of the rewards of making wine.

Adjusting by Blending. What most winemakers strive for is a finished product that is balanced: It is neither thick and syrupy nor thin and bodiless; it is not too intense in flavor or too dull; it is neither too sweet nor so dry that it makes you pucker. It is not too acid or too harsh, but it has enough acid and tannin to give it zest. The color and bouquet should be pleasant, but not overdone.

If you make an unbalanced wine, blending it with another wine that's weak in the opposite direction can greatly improve both — and you will have twice as much good wine. Blending works only when both wines are essentially good wines, wines that fall short by just a little. If you blend a bad or deteriorating wine with any other wine, you'll just end up with a whole lot of bad wine.

Until you become comfortable with blending wines, here are a few pointers. First, don't look for strange new combinations. Confine your blending to wines of the same type — red wines with reds, white wines with whites.

Second, don't just dump two batches of wine together — if you hate the blend, you'll have gallons of the stuff to contend with. Instead, blend a little at a time and keep track of the proportions — 1 part red wine A with 2 parts red wine B, for example. We sometimes use shot glasses as a measure and experiment until we find just the right combination, determined by lots of tasting. Once we decide on the best proportions, we then blend the whole batch and return it to the fermentation vessels. Blended wines almost always ferment again, but gently and only for a couple of days. When the bubbles stop rising, bottle the wine. It will be even better after it has aged for at least six months.

Q A
CAN WINE BOTTLES OR CORKS BE REUSED? WHAT ABOUT REUSING WINE BOTTLES THAT HAVE SCREW CAPS?

Wine bottles can be reused as long as you're careful to sterilize them beforehand. The same is true for corks; you can sterilize corks in a solution of one Campden tablet dissolved in a gallon of water, or by scalding them briefly with boiling water. In our experience, though, corks that are sterilized with bleach or by lengthy boiling absorb either the taste of the bleach or a good deal of water. Corks that have gone "fat" with absorbed water are next to impossible to insert in bottles. Since corks are cheap and readily available, we recommend that you use new corks whenever you make wine.

The screw caps on bottles are usually sealed as well as tightened. If you reuse a screw cap and it leaks air for the time that your wine is aging, you may find that you've been "penny-wise and pound-foolish" because your wine may oxidize, or turn to vinegar. For the few pennies that new corks cost, they are well worth the investment.

Step Six: Stabilize, Bottle, Cellar

Once you have a cleared and sparkling wine, you'll want to make sure that it continues to improve with age. That means that you will need to take as much care with bottling and storing your wine as you did with making it.

Stabilizing Wine. There are essentially two ways to stabilize your wines once they are finished. You can add more alcohol for greater preservative action — a process called fortifying a wine. We don't recommend that method because it can change the flavors you've worked so hard to create. The second way is to add 1 crushed Campden tablet per gallon (3.8 L) of finished wine (even if you already added one to the must). Remember that the effects of the Campden tablet you initially added dissipated after 24 hours.

Adding sulfur dioxide through the use of Campden tablets kills any live yeasts or bacteria that may have entered the wine during racking. Some sulfites will remain in the wine, of course — about 50 parts per million — an important consideration if you're one of those folks whose noses get stuffy after drinking wine. Even a very small amount is enough to cause an allergic reaction in a sensitive person. Almost all commercial wines have added sulfites as a preservative. After sulfites received a lot of bad press, however, commercial winemakers were required to include "contains sulfites" labels to warn the small number of people with sulfite allergies. Be sure to let your guests know if your wines have added sulfites — in very rare cases, a sulfite allergy can cause a dangerous or even deadly reaction. Be aware, also, that sulfites occur naturally in many wines. Few are sulfite-free.

Bottling. When fermentation is complete, use your plastic racking tubes to fill up sterilized bottles. A full bottle should have very little air space left once the cork is inserted. If you've stabilized the wine with a Campden tablet, you've killed any remaining yeast and don't have to worry about continued fermentation building up pressure in the bottles and causing an explosion. Those who don't stabilize their wines should use a hydrometer to measure and calculate the alcohol content and amount of sugar in their wine before bottling; this way, they can be sure that fermentation is complete and bottling is safe.

Q A IS IT HARMFUL TO AGE YOUR WINE IN THE FERMENTATION VESSEL AS LONG AS YOU KEEP THE AIRLOCK ON THE CONTAINER?

Some winemakers never bottle their wines. They simply leave the finished wine in an airlocked fermentation vessel until they are ready to serve it, then siphon the appropriate quantity into a carafe. This way they are never faced with the what-do-I-do-with-a-half-bottle-of-wine dilemma. The problem with handling wine this way is that you need a number of large containers, and whenever you want to make more wine, you must locate additional fermentation vessels. Sometimes big containers are more difficult to store than smaller ones, too. Finally, wine is more likely to oxidize in a large container if it is not used fairly quickly, because every time you remove wine from a container, that amount is replaced with air. If any lees remain in the container, allowing your wine to sit on the sediment for long periods could adversely affect the wine's flavor. For all these reasons, we don't recommend storing wine in the fermentation vessel.

Most winemakers, however, routinely take additional precautions to ensure against exploding bottles. If you are not sure that fermentation is complete, move your wine to a warm room and watch for bubbles, especially along the sides of the container. If no bubbles appear in 24 hours, your wine is finished. If you see any bubbles, wait two weeks to a month and try again. When you don't see any bubbles, put the wine into bottles.

If you end up with not enough wine to fill the last bottle, there are several things you can do to prevent that wine from oxidizing from the air left in the bottle. The easiest way to handle the problem is by topping off. Simply take the wine from several bottles, add enough simple syrup (made by boiling 1 part sugar with 3 parts water) to make enough wine to completely fill the bottles, and return the mixture to an airlocked fermentation vessel until it stops re-fermenting. Then bottle the resulting wine. If you'd rather not bother with the topping-off process, just add the leftover wine to another compatible batch.

Q A CAN YOU PROCESS WINES IN CANNING JARS AS YOU DO FRUITS AND VEGETABLES?

Some commercial winemakers pasteurize wines — though not at canner temperatures — to improve their shipping and keeping qualities. This is rarely done with vintage varieties, however. For the home winemaker, processing wines as you might canned goods is never a good idea. First of all, it just isn't necessary. The alcohol in your wine is an effective preservative, and your homemade wines will not be shipped and jostled and subjected to widely fluctuating temperatures. Even more important, though, processing wine in a hot-water bath or pressure cooker will surely result in most, if not all, of the alcohol evaporating, because alcohol boils at a lower temperature than water. Finally, makers of vintage wines do not pasteurize their wines because they know that fine wines are alive. The aging process that refines and mellows fine wines would stop if the wine were subjected to very high temperatures. Make sure to keep your equipment and bottling supplies sterile, and you will have no need for further processing.

If you make wine in small quantities, it is probably not economical to invest in corking equipment, and there is really no need to do so. Just make sure your bottles and corks are sterile and of compatible sizes. Insert a new cork only one fourth of the way into the bottle's neck so it will pop out rather than break the bottle if you misjudged whether fermentation has ended. If cork-popping becomes too vigorous, the wine probably should be returned to an airlocked vessel for another month or so. After several days with no cork-popping, put several layers of heavy cardboard over the cork (to avoid chipping the bottle neck) and tap it into place with a mallet.

Cellaring. Because wine improves with age, it should always be cellared, or stored, for a time before it is sampled. Our recipes specify different storage times, depending on the kind of wine. Winemakers probably say "Cellar the wine" instead of "Store the wine in a cool, dark place" because it's shorter and fairly descriptive of the kinds of conditions that are best for long-term storage. Be sure to label each bottle before you store it. The cellar location has to remain under 75°F (24°C). At higher temperatures, the wine will oxidize. It is also important to the wine's aging process that the temperature range does not vary greatly (fewer than 10° annually). Finally, the location must be out of direct sunlight, which can cause off-flavors.

Traditionally, wine bottles are stored on their sides, ideally in a rack that allows the corked end of the bottles to tilt slightly downward. Most winemakers use corks when they bottle their wines, and corks can dry out and shrink over long periods in storage. When you store wine bottles on their sides with the mouth of the bottle slightly lower than the bottom, the cork is kept moist and swollen, preventing air from seeping into the bottle and causing oxidation or spoilage.

Storing wine bottles

Storing wine on its side with the neck of the bottle slightly lower than the bottom keeps the cork moist and tight.

Q&A

Q **A** I SOMETIMES GET SOME WHITE, CRYSTAL-TYPE SEDIMENT IN MY WINE. WHAT IS IT AND IS IT DANGEROUS?

The crystals are probably tartaric acid crystals that sometimes form when your wine gets chilled. They are not dangerous and do not affect the wine's taste. If they bother you, rack the wine to leave them behind, but only if you've chilled the wine. If you let your wine warm up too much, the crystals will dissolve back into the wine. Then if you chill the wine before it is served, the crystals will probably form again.

Most of our wild wines are best if used within three to four years after bottling, but they will keep indefinitely if the corks stay tight and the temperatures are cool and constant. Acidity and astringency usually diminish as a wine ages, so aging — up to a point — is good for wine. After too long, however, we think the wines pass their peak and start to taste thin or flat.

Step Seven: Open the Wine and Enjoy!

Removing the cork from your first bottle of a batch of homemade wine is exciting. You've captured "time in a bottle." You'll want to make sure your opening technique keeps the wine inside fresh and appealing. There are dozens of kinds of corkscrews, and most work well. Do be careful, however, to avoid inserting the corkscrew completely through the cork or you will be dismayed to find tiny bits of cork marring the appearance and texture of your wine.

Serving. Some people think that certain wines, especially reds, improve if the bottle is opened a half hour or so before the wine is served at room temperature. That allows any gases that may have collected in the bottle to dissipate. White wines, which are usually fresher tasting than reds, do not need to breathe and should be chilled before serving.

Tasting. If you've ever watched wine tasters in action, you've noticed that they always follow a precise ritual. First, they hold the wineglass up to the light to look at the color and clarity. Sometimes they have a lighted candle for that purpose; they want to be able to see the candle, undistorted, through the wine. They may swirl the wine in the glass and hold it under their noses to enjoy the bouquet — the perfume — which is part of the enjoyment of savoring fine wines. They may also look to see if a bit of the wine clings to the sides of the glass — whether it has what tasters call "legs," a term applied when wine seems to climb up the sides of the glass. Legs are an inexact gauge of a wine's alcohol content. A wine's viscosity, or body, is evaluated partly by a look at the legs and partly by the way the wine feels in the mouth. As you start to look for these things in your own wines, you'll notice a great deal of variability in body, depending on the kind of wine you've made.

Once wine tasters have looked at and smelled the wine, they are ready to taste it. Good wines are generally "balanced" in their taste — with sweet wines, for example, needing a bit more acid and perhaps some more tannin to balance the sugar than drier wines. Most of the terms used to describe taste are self-explanatory — fruity, light, heavy, resinous, sweet, semisweet, semidry, dry, and brut (very dry). A common taste-related term that has a less obvious meaning is "foxy," which is applied to wines with an easily recognizable "grape" taste. Many wine experts who are eager to tell us what wines should taste like often see foxiness as a fault — a mark of inferior quality. But as more and more people become familiar with the variety of wines available — both imported and domestic — they also become more confident wine drinkers. A good wine is one that pleases the drinker, whether it's a foxy grape wine or a mellow cherry melomel.

 CAN I DISTILL MY WINE?

If you mean is it possible to do so, the answer is yes. But if you mean is it legal, the answer is no. And if you mean is it safe, the answer is a resounding no. Distilling may concentrate the methanol that is present in small quantities in wines. At concentrated levels, methanol blinds and kills. Fermented beverages like wine and beer are perfectly safe; distilled beverages must be produced under controlled conditions and tested.

For the best quality, wine should be consumed shortly after it is opened. Oxidation begins quite soon, especially in wines that are not very acid. For that reason, some winemakers avoid bottling their wines in large containers, unless they are intended for a party at which a large number of people are likely to be present. We have stored white wines in the refrigerator for a day or two with little detrimental effect, but as red wines are most often served at room temperature, we try to avoid having partial bottles of the reds. You can store red wine in the refrigerator, of course, but then you'll have to warm it up to room temperature again so it can develop its full flavor. We think repeated chilling and warming has a negative effect on the flavor of red wine.

Chapter Two

MAKING WINES FROM FRUITS

Lining up bottles of colorful homemade wines in your cellar or pantry is especially rewarding if you have harvested the fruit from your own berry patch or orchard. The wines in this chapter have the homey charm of sparkling homemade jams and jellies and fresh-baked fruit pies.

All of our recipes assume the use of fresh fruit at its peak — ripe to perfection, unblemished, and free of bruises. Overripe fruit is not the only problem: The greener the fruit, the higher the pectin content, and the greater the potential for cloudy wine. That's why all recipes call for pectic enzyme. For those few recipes using canned or dried fruits, we specify quantities.

More than most other kinds of wines, those with a fruit component are susceptible to bacterial contamination. That's because fruit flies that carry bacteria are attracted to spoiling fruit. Keep your wines well covered or airlocked at all times, and if you see fruit flies in your home, delay making wine until they are gone.

Dry Apple Wine

Apple wines delighted our ancestors because they represented an economical way to preserve the abundance of fruit that a standard-size apple tree usually produced. This first recipe makes a dry table wine.

YIELD: 1 GALLON (3.8 L)

5 pints (2.4 L) apple juice (without preservatives)

1 teaspoon (5 g) pectic enzyme

2½ pounds (1.14 kg) sugar

1 tablespoon (15 g) citric acid *or* 2 ounces (60 g) acid blend

1 Campden tablet (optional)

1 package (5–7 g) wine yeast

1 teaspoon (5 g) yeast nutrient

1½ cups (360 ml) apple juice, at room temperature

1. Pour the 5 pints of apple juice into a 2-gallon (7.6 L) plastic bucket or wastebasket, and add the pectic enzyme. Add the sugar and citric acid and enough water to make 1 gallon (3.8 L). Add a Campden tablet to the must, if desired, and let the mixture stand, well covered, for 24 hours.

2. In a jar, make a yeast starter culture by combining the wine yeast, yeast nutrient, and the 1½ cups (360 ml) of apple juice. Cover, shake vigorously, and let stand 1 to 3 hours, until bubbly; then add to the must.

3. Let the primary fermentation occur in the fermentation vat for 48 hours, stirring with a clean plastic or metal spoon twice a day to aerate the mixture. Then, using a wire strainer lined with two or three layers of cheesecloth, strain the mixture into an airlocked fermentation vessel. Discard the solids. Allow the mixture to ferment for three to six months. When fermentation is complete, rack the wine into bottles.

4. Wait at least six months before opening your first bottle.

VARIATION: Cinnamon-Apple Wine

Reduce the sugar by 2 tablespoons (30 g) and add an equal amount of small, red cinnamon candies.

Medium-Sweet Apple Wine

Apple wines are mellow, golden, and likely to be something of a surprise, depending on the variety of fruit you use. Some apples, like Jonathans, have spicy components; others, like Golden Delicious, are mild. Even canned apple juices will vary in taste, depending on the brand.

YIELD: 1 GALLON (3.8 L)

6 to 8 pounds (2.7–3.6 kg) ripe apples

1 pound (450 g) light raisins

1 teaspoon (5 g) pectic enzyme

1 tablespoon (15 g) citric acid *or* 2 ounces (60 g) acid blend

1 Campden tablet (optional)

1 package (5–7 g) wine yeast

1 teaspoon (5 g) yeast nutrient

1½ cups (360 ml) orange juice, at room temperature

1. Crush the apples and combine with the raisins in a 2-gallon (7.6 L) plastic container. Add the pectic enzyme, the acid, and enough water to make 1 gallon (3.8 L). Add a Campden tablet, if desired, and let the mixture stand for 24 hours, well covered, stirring once or twice. Strain out the solids by placing the mixture in a bag and pressing out the juices in a fruit press. Discard the solids.

2. In a jar, make a yeast starter culture by combining the wine yeast, yeast nutrient, and orange juice. Cover, shake vigorously, and let stand 1 to 3 hours, until bubbly; then add to the must.

3. Filter the juice through cheesecloth into an airlocked fermentation vessel. Ferment for three months initially, then rack the wine into bottles.

4. Age in the bottles for an additional six to twelve months.

VARIATION: Apple-Almond Dessert Wine
Add ¼ cup (112 g) chopped, toasted almonds with the crushed apples and raisins.

Spiced Apple Wine

This is a delightfully spicy wine for those cold winter nights when a little warmth is welcome.

YIELD: 1 GALLON (3.8 L)

2½ pounds (1.14 kg) clover honey

36 ounces (1.1 L) apple juice concentrate

1 Campden tablet (optional)

1 package (5–7 g) wine yeast

1 teaspoon (5 g) yeast nutrient

1 teaspoon (5 g) pectic enzyme

¼ teaspoon (1.25 g) tannin

½ teaspoon (2.5 g) ground cloves

½ teaspoon (2.5 g) ground nutmeg

1 cinnamon stick

12 allspice berries, crushed

1 vanilla bean

Apple juice or simple syrup for topping off

1. Mix the honey with ½ gallon (1.9 L) of water in a medium saucepan. Bring the mixture to a boil, skimming off the foam. Let cool and stir in the apple juice concentrate. Add the Campden tablet, if desired, cover tightly with aluminum foil, and let stand for 24 hours.

2. In a jar, make a yeast starter culture by combining the wine yeast, yeast nutrient, and about 1½ cups (360 ml) of the apple juice–honey mixture. Cover, shake vigorously, and let stand 1 to 3 hours, until bubbly; then add it to the fermentation vessel along with the remainder of the apple juice–honey mixture, pectic enzyme, and tannin.

3. Let this mixture ferment for one month; then rack the wine, leaving any sediment behind. Add the spices, top off the container with preservative-free apple juice or simple syrup, and ferment for another month. Rack the mixture again, removing the spices from the wine. Let the mixture stand for one more month before bottling.

4. Cellar the wine for six months before sampling.

Crab Apple Wine

Crab apples are great for making wine. The color of the wine will vary from golden to faintly pink, depending on how you treat the apples and their degree of ripeness. Be sure to include pectic enzyme in crab apple wine. The green apples are especially high in pectin and likely to produce a cloudy wine without treatment.

YIELD: 1 GALLON (3.8 L)

2 pounds (900 g) white sugar

3 pounds (1.4 kg) crab apples, cut into medium dice

2 pounds (900 g) green apples, cut into medium dice

1 Campden tablet (optional)

1 package (5–7 g) wine yeast

12 ounces (360 ml) apple juice concentrate

1 tablespoon (15 g) white sugar

1 teaspoon (5 g) pectic enzyme

1 teaspoon (5 g) yeast nutrient

¼ teaspoon (1.25 g) tannin

1. In a medium pot, bring ½ gallon (1.9 L) of water and the 2 pounds (900 g) of sugar to a boil. Place the crab apples and the green apples in a clean, sterile fermentation vessel. Pour the sugar water over the fruit, add the Campden tablet, if desired, and let stand, tightly covered, for 24 hours.

2. In a jar, make a yeast starter culture by combining the wine yeast, 2 tablespoons (30 ml) of the apple juice concentrate, the 1 tablespoon (15 ml) of sugar, and ½ cup (120 ml) of warm water. Add the starter culture, pectic enzyme, yeast nutrient, tannin, and the juice concentrate to the must. Stir the mixture daily to keep the pulp cap moist. Let stand for one week.

3. Rack the liquid into an airlocked fermentation vessel and ferment for one month; then rack again. Top off the mixture with preservative-free apple juice, if necessary, and let stand for one month. Rack again, repeating the topping-off process. In three to four months the fermentation should be complete.

4. Bottle and cellar the wine, and wait about six months before opening.

VARIATION: Crabby Cranberry Wine

Reduce the water by 1 cup (240 ml) and add an equal amount of cranberry juice.

Apple Cider Wine

This smooth, golden wine will probably be the mellowest apple wine you make, largely because cider usually comes from a blend of apple varieties, so the acid component tends to be balanced. Also, apples used for cider are usually fully ripe, and thus have lost most of their tartness.

YIELD: 1 GALLON (3.8 L)

1½ pounds (675 g) clover honey

Juice of 1 orange

Juice of 1 lemon

1 teaspoon (5 g) pectic enzyme

¼ teaspoon (1.25 g) tannin

3 quarts (2.8 L) fresh, preservative-free apple cider

1 Campden tablet (optional)

1 package (5–7 g) wine yeast

1 teaspoon (5 g) yeast nutrient

1. Boil the clover honey in 1 quart (about 1 L) of water in a saucepan over medium heat. Skim off the foam and discard. Let cool. Add the orange juice, lemon juice, pectic enzyme, and tannin to the honey mixture and pour into an airlocked vessel. Add the apple cider. Add the Campden tablet, if desired, and allow the mixture to stand, covered, for 24 hours.

2. In a jar, make a yeast starter culture by combining the wine yeast and yeast nutrient with about 1½ cups (360 ml) of the apple cider–honey mixture. Shake the mixture daily for two weeks; then rack the must into another clean, airlocked vessel. Rack again after one month and then top off with water. Let stand for three more months; then rack and bottle.

3. Cellar the wine for six months before sampling.

APPLE WINE TIP: Because underripe apples are high in pectin, and pectin makes wines difficult to clear, be very careful to choose fully ripe apples. Even then it's a good idea to add pectic enzyme to all apple wines. We usually make apple wines late in the fall, when the fruit is readily available and inexpensive.

Apricot Wine

The apricot's intense flavor becomes mellow and full-bodied in wine. The lovely golden color is a plus.

YIELD: 1 GALLON (3.8 L)

3 pounds (1.4 kg) fresh apricots

1½ pounds (675 g) sugar

1 pound (450 g) honey

1 pound (450 g) high-quality dried apricots,* chopped

Juice of 2 lemons

1 teaspoon (5 g) lemon zest

¼ teaspoon (1.25 g) tannin

1 teaspoon (5 g) yeast nutrient

1 teaspoon (5 g) pectic enzyme

1 Campden tablet (optional)

1 package (5–7 g) wine yeast

1. Cut fresh apricots in half, remove pits, and cut the fruit into quarters. Put the fruit in a plastic bucket or wastebasket and cover with the sugar. Mix ½ gallon (1.9 L) of water with the honey in a saucepan and bring to a boil. Skim off the foam. When no more foam rises to the top, add the chopped dried apricots to the honey mixture and pour it over the fresh apricots. Add the lemon juice, lemon zest, tannin, yeast nutrient, pectic enzyme, and Campden tablet (if desired) to the mixture. Let stand for 24 hours.

2. Add the yeast and let mixture ferment for one week, stirring daily. Remove the solids and pour the liquid into an airlocked fermentation vessel. Let ferment for one month. Rack again and let ferment for two months. Rack again; then bottle, cork, and cellar the wine.

3. Wait at least six months before sampling.

*Dried apricots are often treated with sulfites, so be sure to follow the above directions precisely.

Blackberry Wine

In those parts of the country where blackberries grow wild, finding their trailing canes along fencerows once meant that luscious jellies and delicious wines were in the offing. A tablespoon of blackberry cordial was my great-grandfather's favorite cold remedy. Having tasted these luscious blackberry country wines, I can see why my grandma still remembers her girlhood cold remedy with affection, even after more than 90 years!

YIELD: 1 GALLON (3.8 L)

3½ pounds (1.6 kg) ripe blackberries

1 Campden tablet (optional)

1 teaspoon (5 g) pectic enzyme

1 package (5–7 g) wine yeast

1 teaspoon (5 g) yeast nutrient

1½ cups (360 ml) orange juice, at room temperature

2¼ pounds (1 kg) sugar

1. Wash the berries carefully; and then crush them in a 2-gallon (7.6 L) sterilized plastic fermentation vat or wastebasket. Add a Campden tablet, if desired, and let stand, well covered, for 24 hours. Pour 2 quarts (1.9 L) of boiling water over the mixture and let cool; then add the pectic enzyme.

2. In a jar, make a yeast starter culture by combining the wine yeast, yeast nutrient, and orange juice. Cover, shake vigorously, and let stand 1 to 3 hours, until bubbly. Then add to the must.

3. Cover the container with plastic wrap or aluminum foil and let stand for four or five days. Strain the mixture through cheesecloth and dissolve the sugar in the resulting juice. Add enough water to make 1 gallon (3.8 L). Pour the mixture into an airlocked fermentation vessel and let the wine clear. Rack the mixture into a sterilized jar. Taste for sweetness; stir in more sugar, up to ¾ pound (340 g), if necessary. Siphon the mixture into an airlocked vessel to complete the fermentation. Rack the wine again and bottle it.

4. Wait at least six months before opening your first bottle.

Sweet Port-Style Blackberry Wine

Pretty is as pretty does — and this very pretty, dark red to purple wine does just fine, thank you. Ripe blackberries are sweet and mellow, so the acid components and tannins are very important to this wine's balance.

YIELD: 1 GALLON (3.8 L)

7 pounds (3.2 kg) blackberries

4 pounds (1.8 kg) sugar

1 Campden tablet (optional)

⅛ teaspoon (.625 g) tannin *or* 1 tablespoon (15 ml) strong tea

1 package (5–7 g) port wine yeast

1 teaspoon (5 g) yeast nutrient

½ cup (120 ml) white grape juice, at room temperature

Juice of 1 orange

1 orange rind, grated

1. In a large mixing bowl, crush all the berries a few at a time. Transfer the berries to a plastic fermentation vat or clean plastic wastebasket, and add half the sugar and 3 quarts (2.8 L) of water. Add a Campden tablet to kill any wild yeast that may be present on the fruit, if you desire. (If you do, let the mixture stand for 24 hours, well covered, before proceeding.) Add the rest of the sugar, the tannin, and enough water to make 1 gallon (3.8 L).

2. In a jar, make a yeast starter culture by combining the wine yeast, yeast nutrient, and grape juice. Cover, shake vigorously, and let stand 1 to 3 hours, until bubbly; then add to the must.

3. Ferment the mixture for two days, and then rack. Add the orange juice and the grated rind (avoiding the white inner rind). Ferment this mixture for five days. Rack the wine to clarify it, and let it sit for five more days. Rack into an airlocked fermentation vessel and allow the wine to ferment to completion. When you are sure that the fermentation is done, bottle, cork, and cellar the wine.

4. Wait at least six months before opening your first bottle.

Blueberry Wine

This recipe uses wild blueberries, which give the wine an added piquancy. But you can choose from a number of domesticated varieties of berry that also result in a delicious wine. As with all wines, use whatever variety is most available and economical in your area.

YIELD: 1 GALLON (3.8 L)

1 gallon (3.8 L) blueberries

3 pounds (1.4 kg) sugar

1 Campden tablet (optional)

1 teaspoon (5 g) acid blend

¼ teaspoon (1.25 g) tannin

1 package (5–7 g) wine yeast

1 teaspoon (5 g) yeast nutrient

1½ cups (360 ml) blueberry juice, at room temperature

1. In a large mixing bowl, crush the berries a few at a time. Transfer the berries to a plastic fermentation vat or clean plastic wastebasket, and add half the sugar and 3 quarts (2.8 L) of water. Add a Campden tablet to kill any wild yeast that may be present on the fruit, if you desire. (If you do, let the mixture stand for 24 hours, well covered, before proceeding.) Add the rest of the sugar, the tannin, and enough water to make 1 gallon (3.8 L).

2. In a jar, make a yeast starter culture by combining the wine yeast, yeast nutrient, and blueberry juice. Cover, shake vigorously, and let stand 1 to 3 hours, until bubbly. Then add to the must.

3. Ferment the mixture for two days. Rack the wine to clarify it, and let it sit for five more days. Rack into an airlocked fermentation vessel and allow the wine to ferment to completion. When you are sure that the fermentation is done, bottle, cork, and cellar the wine.

4. Wait at least six months before opening your first bottle.

VARIATION: Spiced Blueberry Wine

In step 1, add a bundle of spices, tied in a coffee filter, to the must. Cinnamon and nutmeg work well.

Cherry Dessert Wine

Cherry wines are a delight to your senses. The color is gorgeous, the aroma is tantalizing, and the flavor is delightfully fresh. This isn't a wine to serve with dessert — it is dessert.

YIELD: 1 GALLON (3.8 L)

2 pounds (900 g) dark red sweet cherries, pitted

3 pounds (1.4 kg) tart pie cherries, pitted

2 pounds (900 g) white sugar

1 pound (450 g) clover honey

12 ounces (360 ml) preservative-free apple juice concentrate

6 ounces (180 ml) tangerine juice concentrate

1 teaspoon (5 g) orange zest

¼ teaspoon (1.25 g) tannin

1 teaspoon (5 g) yeast nutrient

1 teaspoon (5 g) pectic enzyme

1 Campden tablet (optional)

1 package (5–7 g) wine yeast

1. On a cutting board, coarsely chop the sweet and tart cherries. Transfer them to a 2-gallon (7.6 L) plastic bucket or wastebasket, and cover with the sugar. Set aside.

2. In a saucepan, mix ½ gallon (1.9 L) of water with the honey and bring to a boil, skimming off the foam. When no more foam rises to the top, add the apple and tangerine concentrates to the mixture and stir to blend. Pour the mixture over the cherries. Add the orange zest, tannin, yeast nutrient, pectic enzyme, and Campden tablet (if desired), and let stand for 24 hours.

3. Add the wine yeast. Let the mixture ferment for one week, stirring daily. Remove the solids and pour the liquid into an airlocked fermentation vessel. Let ferment for one month. Rack again and let ferment for two months. Rack again; then bottle, cork, and cellar the wine.

4. Wait six months before sampling.

VARIATION: Fortified Cherry Wine

You can fortify this wine by adding 1 cup (240 ml) of a good-quality brandy before bottling.

Dry Cherry Wine

We keep experimenting with cherry wines because the results are always better than we expect them to be. Here is a recipe for a dry version.

YIELD: 1 GALLON (3.8 L)

3½ pounds (1.6 kg) tart pie cherries, pitted

2¼ pounds (1 kg) white sugar

6 ounces (180 ml) tangerine juice concentrate

1 teaspoon (5 g) orange zest

¼ teaspoon (1.25 g) tannin

1 teaspoon (5 g) yeast nutrient

1 teaspoon (5 g) pectic enzyme

1 Campden tablet (optional)

1 package (5–7 g) wine yeast

1. In a medium bowl, coarsely chop the cherries and transfer them to a plastic bucket or wastebasket. In a medium saucepan, mix ½ gallon (1.9 L) of water with the sugar and bring to a boil. Add the tangerine juice concentrate and pour the mixture over the cherries. Let stand for ½ hour. Add the orange zest, tannin, yeast nutrient, pectic enzyme, and Campden tablet (if desired) to the mixture. Let stand for 24 hours.

2. Add the yeast and let the mixture ferment for one week, stirring daily. Remove the solids and discard. Place the liquid into an airlocked fermentation vessel and let ferment for one month. Rack again and let ferment for two months. Rack again; then bottle, cork, and cellar the wine.

3. Wait at least six months before sampling.

VARIATION: Cherry Almond Wine
In step 1, add ¼ cup (112 g) chopped, toasted almonds to the sugar–water mixture before boiling.

Cranberry Claret

Tart, acidic cranberries may not suit your taste for good eating, but you will love what they do to wines. The fermentation process mellows the sharp flavors, and the color is beautifully clear and sparkling.

YIELD: 1 GALLON (3.8 L)

3 pounds (1.4 kg) fresh cranberries

2 pounds (900 g) white sugar

1 pound (450 g) clover honey

Juice of 2 large oranges

2 teaspoons (10 g) orange zest

8 ounces (240 g) golden raisins

¼ teaspoon (1.25 g) tannin

1 teaspoon (5 g) yeast nutrient

1 teaspoon (5 g) pectic enzyme

1 Campden tablet (optional)

1 package (5–7 g) wine yeast

1. Wash and sort the cranberries, removing any that are blemished or spoiled. Coarsely chop the berries in a blender or food processor. Transfer the cranberries into a 2-gallon (7.6 L) plastic bucket or wastebasket, and cover them with the sugar.

2. In a medium saucepan, mix the honey with ½ gallon (1.9 L) of water and bring to a boil. Skim off any foam that appears. When no more foam rises to the top, pour the honey–water mixture over the cranberries. Add the orange juice, zest, raisins, tannin, yeast nutrient, pectic enzyme, and Campden tablet (if desired) to the mixture. Let stand for 24 hours.

3. Add the yeast and let the mixture ferment for one week, stirring daily. Remove the solids and discard. Pour the liquid into an airlocked fermentation vessel and let ferment for one month. Rack again and let ferment for two months. Rack again; then bottle, cork, and cellar the wine.

4. Wait six months before sampling.

Gooseberry Wine

Pluck a plump green gooseberry off the bush, pop it into your mouth, and be prepared to pucker up. With this pursed and pained expression on your face, people might think you're pondering some deep philosophical problem, and you are: You are wondering what perversity might inspire anyone to make wine from such an astringent and disagreeable little berry. But Grandma knew that something magic happened to gooseberries when she added enough sugar and tucked them between two slabs of flaky homemade pastry. And Grandpa, not to be outdone, discovered that a little sugar and fermentation certainly improved the unadorned berry. You have to age gooseberry wine for at least a year, but we bet you'll think it was worth the wait.

YIELD: 1 GALLON (3.8 L)

5 pounds (2.3 kg) ripe green gooseberries

1 teaspoon (5 g) pectic enzyme

1 Campden tablet (optional)

1 package (5–7 g) wine yeast

1 teaspoon (5 g) yeast nutrient

1½ cups (360 ml) orange juice, at room temperature

2 pounds (900 g) sugar

1. Remove the stems and tails of the gooseberries and wash the fruit, making sure the berries are completely clean. Put them into a 2-gallon (7.6 L) plastic fermentation vat or wastebasket, and squeeze them by hand until they are pulpy. Add the pectic enzyme and enough water to make 1 gallon (3.8 L). Add the Campden tablet, if desired, and wait 24 hours.

2. In a small jar, make a yeast starter culture by combining the wine yeast, yeast nutrient, and orange juice. Cover, shake vigorously, and let stand 1 to 3 hours, until bubbly; then add to the must.

3. Cover the container with plastic wrap or aluminum foil and let stand for three days, stirring three or four times. Strain out the solids and add the sugar. Put the mixture into an airlocked fermentation vessel and let stand until it stops bubbling. Rack the wine into an airlocked container and leave it to mature for about six months. Rack into bottles, cork them, and cellar your wine.

4. Age the wine for at least one year after bottling.

Huckleberry Wine

Finding enough wild huckleberries to satisfy the needs of both pie- and winemaking must have been tough in the days before garden huckleberries became widely available. Fortunately, the children of a bygone era seemed to regard wild-berry picking as a treat. If a large family pooled their gleanings, they probably had enough berries for both endeavors. Huckleberries make a light, dry wine that complements fowl and seafood.

YIELD: 1 GALLON (3.8 L)

1 gallon (3.8 L) huckleberries

3 pounds (1.4 kg) sugar

1 Campden tablet (optional)

1 teaspoon (5 g) acid blend *or* the juice of 3 citrus fruits

¼ teaspoon (1.25 g) tannin *or* 1 tablespoon (15 ml) strong tea

1 package (5–7 g) wine yeast

1 teaspoon (5 g) yeast nutrient

1½ cups (360 ml) orange juice, at room temperature

1. In a medium bowl, crush all the berries, a few at a time. Transfer the crushed berries, half the sugar, and 3 quarts (2.8 L) of water to a plastic fermentation vat or clean plastic wastebasket. Add a Campden tablet to kill any wild yeast that may be present on the fruit, if you desire. (If you do, let the mixture stand for 24 hours, well covered, before proceeding.) Add the rest of the sugar, the acid blend, tannin, and enough water to make 1 gallon (3.8 L).

2. In a small jar, make a yeast starter culture by combining the wine yeast, yeast nutrient, and orange juice. Cover, shake vigorously, and let stand 1 to 3 hours, until bubbly; then add to the must.

3. Ferment the mixture for two days; then rack the wine to clarify it. Let it sit for five more days. Rack into an airlocked fermentation vessel and allow the wine to ferment to completion. When you are sure that the fermentation is done, bottle, cork, and cellar the wine.

4. Wait at least six months before opening your first bottle.

Loganberry Wine

Boysenberries and loganberries are large, wine-colored berries of the blackberry family. Because these varieties are available only in certain sections of the country, you can substitute any of the blackberry family members and get a perfectly delicious wine. If you use canned loganberries, there will be no difference in the amount needed.

YIELD: 1 GALLON (3.8 L)

2½ pounds (1.14 kg) fresh loganberries

1 teaspoon (5 g) pectic enzyme

1 teaspoon (5 g) acid blend

1 cup (240 ml) grape juice concentrate

2½ pounds (1.14 kg) sugar

1 Campden tablet (optional)

1 package (5–7 g) wine yeast

1 teaspoon (5 g) yeast nutrient

1½ cups (360 ml) orange juice, at room temperature

1. Crush the loganberries in a 2-gallon (7.6 L) plastic bucket or wastebasket. Pour 2 quarts (1.9 L) of boiling water over them and let the mixture cool. Add the pectic enzyme, acid blend, and grape juice concentrate; cover the container with plastic wrap or foil.

2. Let stand for four or five days, stirring daily. Strain the liquid through cheesecloth, discard the solids, and add the sugar to the liquid, stirring to dissolve. Add a Campden tablet, if desired, and let sit for 24 hours, well covered, before proceeding.

3. In a small jar, make a yeast starter culture by combining the wine yeast, yeast nutrient, and orange juice. Cover, shake vigorously, and let stand 1 to 3 hours, until bubbly; then add to the must.

4. Add enough water to make 1 gallon (3.8 L), and pour the liquid into an airlocked fermentation vessel. Let the wine complete the fermentation process. When it is clear, rack, bottle, and cellar the wine.

5. Wait for at least six months before opening your first bottle.

Sweet Mulberry Wine

Anyone who has a mulberry tree in the yard knows that these berries can be a real pain in the neck. The fruit falls all summer, creating disagreeable purple stains on the patio, shoes, and children's clothes. When you do gather enough to make something of them, the stems are difficult to remove and you end up with purple fingers and meager results. In fact, as far as we can tell, there's only one thing that mulberries are really good for, and that's making wine. Maybe that's why we've found so many mulberry wine recipes. Here is one on the sweet side.

YIELD: 1 GALLON (3.8 L)

5 pounds (2.3 kg) mulberries

1 teaspoon (5 g) pectic enzyme

4 pounds (1.8 kg) sugar

1 Campden tablet (optional)

1 package (5–7 g) wine yeast

1 teaspoon (5 g) yeast nutrient

1½ cups (360 ml) orange juice, at room temperature

1 teaspoon (5 g) acid blend

¼ teaspoon (1.25 g) tannin *or* 1 tablespoon (15 ml) strong tea

1. Crush the mulberries in a 2-gallon (7.6 L) plastic bucket or wastebasket, and pour 2 quarts (1.9 L) of boiling water over them. Let the mixture cool, add the pectic enzyme, and cover the container with plastic wrap or foil. Let stand for four or five days, stirring daily.

2. Strain the liquid through cheesecloth and add the sugar, stirring to dissolve. Add a Campden tablet, if desired, and let sit for 24 hours, well covered, before proceeding.

3. In a jar, make a yeast starter culture by combining the wine yeast, yeast nutrient, and orange juice. Cover, shake vigorously, and let stand 1 to 3 hours, until bubbly; then add to the must.

4. Add the remaining ingredients, plus enough water to make 1 gallon (3.8 L), and pour the liquid into an airlocked fermentation vessel. Let the wine complete the fermentation process. When it is clear, rack and bottle the wine.

5. Wait at least six months before opening your first bottle.

Dry Mulberry Wine

Here is a recipe for a dry wine using these pesky purple berries.

YIELD: 1 GALLON (3.8 L)

3 pounds (1.4 kg) mulberries

1 teaspoon (5 g) pectic enzyme

2½ pounds (1.14 kg) sugar

1 Campden tablet (optional)

1 package (5–7 g) wine yeast

1 teaspoon (5 g) yeast nutrient

1½ cups (360 ml) orange juice, at room temperature

1 pound (450 g) gooseberries *or* 1 pound (450 g) diced green apples *or* 1 pound (450 g) raisins

Juice of 1 orange

1. Crush the mulberries in a 2-gallon (7.6 L) plastic bucket or wastebasket, and pour 2 quarts (1.9 L) of boiling water over them. Let the mixture cool. Add the pectic enzyme, and cover the container with plastic wrap or foil. Let stand for four or five days, stirring daily. Strain the liquid through cheese-cloth and add the sugar, stirring to dissolve. Add a Campden tablet, if desired, and let sit for 24 hours, well covered, before proceeding.

2. In a jar, make a yeast starter culture by combining the wine yeast, yeast nutri-ent, and orange juice. Cover, shake vigorously, and let stand 1 to 3 hours, until bubbly; then add to the must.

3. Add the remaining ingredients, plus enough water to make 1 gallon (3.8 L), and pour the mixture into an airlocked fermentation vessel. Let the wine complete the fermentation process. When it is clear, rack and bottle it.

4. Wait at least six months before opening your first bottle.

COLLECTING MULBERRIES: Spread a large piece of plastic or an old sheet on the ground beneath a mulberry tree and give the branches a good shake. It may take you several days to gather enough berries for a batch of wine. We don't stem the mulberries as carefully as we'd have to for table use, since the solid materials will be strained out after a few days. Just wash the berries carefully, and you're ready to begin.

Pear Wine

If you love the flavor and aroma of fresh pears but dislike the grit, this wine may be the one for you. Pear wine, also sometimes called perry, is especially nice with poultry dishes or fish.

YIELD: 1 GALLON (3.8 L)

4½ pounds (2 kg) ripe pears

1 pound (450 g) sugar

1 pound (450 g) honey

Juice of 2 lemons

1 teaspoon (5 g) lemon zest

¼ teaspoon (1.25 g) tannin

1 teaspoon (5 g) yeast nutrient

1 teaspoon (5 g) pectic enzyme

1 Campden tablet (optional)

1 package (5–7 g) wine yeast

1. Peel, seed, and core the pears, and chop them into 1-inch pieces. Place them in a plastic bucket or wastebasket, and cover with the sugar. Set aside.

2. Mix the honey into ½ gallon (1.9 L) of water, and bring to a boil in a medium saucepan. Skim off any foam that rises to the surface. When no more foam emerges, pour the honey–water mixture over the pears. Add the lemon juice, lemon zest, tannin, yeast nutrient, pectic enzyme, and Campden tablet (if desired). Let stand for 24 hours.

3. Add the yeast and let the mixture ferment for one week, stirring daily. Remove the solids and discard. Pour the liquid into an airlocked fermentation vessel, and let ferment for one month. Rack again and let ferment for two months. Rack again; then bottle, cork, and cellar the wine.

4. Wait at least six months before sampling; then serve chilled.

VARIATION: Spiced Pear Wine

Add a packet of spices — cinnamon and nutmeg work well — to the honey–water mixture before boiling. Tie 1 cinnamon stick and 2 whole nutmeg into a coffee filter and boil. Remove before adding the rest of the ingredients in step 2.

Pineapple-Orange Delight

The color is light, but the flavor is redolent of the tropics. Choose a ripe pineapple, one that will release a leaf of its topknot with a firm tug — or give the pineapple the sniff test. The flavor — and ultimately the bouquet of your wine — will be reflected in the aroma of the pineapple you use.

YIELD: 1 GALLON (3.8 L)

4 pounds (1.8 kg) ripe pineapple

1 tablespoon (15 g) light brown sugar

4 ounces (120 g) golden raisins, chopped

2 pounds (900 g) orange-blossom honey

12 ounces (360 ml) orange juice concentrate

Juice of 1 lemon

1 teaspoon (5 g) orange zest

¼ teaspoon (1.25 g) tannin

1 teaspoon (5 g) yeast nutrient

1 teaspoon (5 g) pectic enzyme

1 Campden tablet (optional)

1 package (5–7 g) wine yeast

1. Chop and core the pineapple, and transfer to a 2-gallon (7.6 L) plastic bucket or wastebasket. Add the sugar and raisins, and set aside.

2. In a medium saucepan, mix the honey in ½ gallon (1.9 L) of water, and bring to a boil. Skim off any foam. When no more foam rises to the top, pour the honey–water mixture over the pineapple mixture. Add the orange juice concentrate, lemon juice, orange zest, tannin, yeast nutrient, pectic enzyme, and Campden tablet (if desired). Let stand for 24 hours.

3. Add the yeast and let the mixture ferment for one week, stirring daily. Remove the solids. Pour the liquid into an airlocked fermentation vessel, and let ferment for one month. Rack again and let ferment for two months. Rack again. When the fermentation is complete, bottle, cork, and cellar the wine.

4. Wait at least six months before sampling.

Black Plum Wine

The finished wine will be dry with a lovely color — one you will be proud to show off.

YIELD: 1 GALLON (3.8 L)

3 pounds (1.4 kg) black (or deep purple) plums

2½ pounds (1.14 kg) sugar

Juice of 2 oranges

¼ teaspoon (1.25 g) tannin

1 teaspoon (5 g) pectic enzyme

1 Campden tablet (optional)

1 package (5–7 g) wine yeast

1 teaspoon (5 g) yeast nutrient

1 teaspoon (5 g) acid blend

1. Cut the plums into quarters, removing the pits. Transfer the fruit to a 2-gallon (7.6 L) plastic bucket or wastebasket; then mash the fruit.

2. In a medium saucepan, mix the sugar in ½ gallon (1.9 L) of water and bring to a boil. Pour the sugar–water mixture over the plums and let cool. Add the orange juice, tannin, pectic enzyme, and Campden tablet (if desired), and let stand for 24 hours.

3. In a jar, make a yeast starter culture by combining the wine yeast, yeast nutrient, and orange juice. Cover, shake vigorously, and let stand 1 to 3 hours, until bubbly; then add to the must.

4. Let the mixture ferment for one week, stirring the cap into the fermenting must daily. Rack the solids from the liquid. Pour the liquid into a sterile air-locked fermentation vessel, and let the mixture ferment for approximately one month. Rack again and let the mixture stand for two more months. Rack for the final time; then bottle, cork, and cellar the wine.

5. Wait three to six months before opening your first bottle.

Golden Plum Wine

Plum wines are perfect with Chinese or Japanese cuisine. Because plums come in a variety of colors, the wines you create from these fruits come in a range of hues. Plums are among the most versatile of native fruit wine ingredients.

YIELD: 1 GALLON (3.8 L)

3½ pounds (1.6 kg) yellow plums

8 ounces (240 g) golden raisins, chopped

2 pounds (900 g) sugar

1 pound (450 g) honey

Juice of 2 oranges

⅛ teaspoon (.625 g) tannin

1 teaspoon (5 g) pectic enzyme

1 Campden tablet (optional)

1 package (5–7 g) wine yeast

1 teaspoon (5 g) yeast nutrient

1. Cut the plums into quarters, removing the pits. In a 2-gallon (7.6 L) plastic bucket or wastebasket, mash them the plums and add the raisins and sugar.

2. In a medium saucepan, mix the honey into ½ gallon (1.9 L) of water and bring the mixture to a boil. Skim off the foam. When no more foam rises to the top, pour the honey–water mixture over the plums and let cool. Add the tannin, pectic enzyme, and Campden tablet (if desired) to the mixture, and let stand for 24 hours.

3. In a jar, make a yeast starter culture by combining the wine yeast, yeast nutrient, and orange juice. Cover, shake vigorously, and let stand 1 to 3 hours, until bubbly; then add to the must.

4. Let this mixture ferment for one week, stirring the cap into the fermenting must daily. Rack the solids from the liquid, and pour the liquid into a sterile airlocked fermentation vessel. Let the mixture ferment for approximately one month. Rack again and let the mixture stand for two more months. Rack for the final time; then bottle, cork, and cellar the wine.

5. Wait three to six months before opening your first bottle.

Quince Wine

This is a nice, dry wine with hints of pear and apple in its flavor. For those who have never seen a quince tree, the fruit is yellow to yellow-green — it resembles a pear in color, though it doesn't have the classic pear shape. (The fruit looks something like a fat doughnut, with depressions where the hole would be on either end.)

YIELD: 1 GALLON (3.8 L)

20 ripe quinces

2¼ pounds (1 kg) sugar

Juice and zest of 2 lemons

1 teaspoon (5 g) pectic enzyme

1 Campden tablet (optional)

1 package (5–7 g) wine yeast

1 teaspoon (5 g) yeast nutrient

1½ cups (360 ml) orange juice, at room temperature

1. Grate the quinces as near to the core as possible. Boil the grated peel and pulp in enough water to cover, for a maximum of 15 minutes. (Don't overcook the fruit or you may have trouble clearing the wine.)

2. Strain the mixture and pour the juice onto the sugar in a bucket or a large plastic wastebasket. Add the juice and zest of the lemons. Let the mixture cool; then add the pectic enzyme. Add a Campden tablet, if desired, and let the mixture sit, well covered, for 24 hours.

3. In a jar, make a yeast starter culture by combining the wine yeast, yeast nutrient, and orange juice. Cover, shake vigorously, and let stand 1 to 3 hours, until bubbly; then add to the must.

4. Add enough water to make 1 gallon (3.8 L), and allow the mixture to ferment for 48 hours. Rack into an airlocked fermentation vessel, and let the wine ferment to completion (about nine months), racking at intervals as needed to clear the wine. When you are sure that fermentation is complete, bottle, cork and cellar the wine.

5. Age for at least six months before sampling.

Raisin Wine

When you are thinking about making wine, it is easy to forget that raisins are just dried grapes. That's why raisin wine is among the easiest of all wines to make. You could make raisin wine from little more than sugar, raisins, and water — and many home winemakers do. But like fresh grapes, raisins carry a number of wild yeasts on their skins, so making wine from just these three ingredients won't give you the same result every time. We usually kill off the resident yeasts and add wine yeast from a known source when we make wine from raisins.

YIELD: 1 GALLON (3.8 L)

1¾ pounds (840 g) large raisins (dark or light)

1¾ pounds (840 g) sugar

1 Campden tablet (optional)

1 teaspoon (5 g) citric acid *or* acid blend

1 teaspoon (5 g) pectic enzyme

1 package (5–7 g) wine yeast

1 teaspoon (5 g) yeast nutrient

1½ cups (360 ml) orange juice, at room temperature

1. In a large, unchipped enamel or stainless steel pot, boil the raisins in 2 quarts (1.9 L) of water for 1 minute. Let the mixture cool to room temperature, and then strain the liquid onto the sugar in a 2-gallon (7.6 L) plastic bucket, wastebasket, or other fermentation vat. Add a Campden tablet, if desired. Let the mixture stand, well covered, for 24 hours. Then add the acid, pectic enzyme, and enough water to make 1 gallon (3.8 L).

2. In a jar, make a yeast starter culture by combining the wine yeast, yeast nutrient, and orange juice. Cover, shake vigorously, and let stand 1 to 3 hours, until bubbly; then add to the must.

3. Pour the mixture into an airlocked fermentation vessel. When the wine has cleared, rack and return to a clean airlocked fermentation vessel. Ferment to completion; then bottle, cork, and cellar the wine.

4. Wait at least six months before sampling.

Dry Raspberry Wine

Delicate, fragile raspberries are the delight of the home garden, mostly because gardeners know that really good raspberries are few and far between in supermarkets. They don't ship well, and even the most generous home growers usually don't have enough to share. If you raise raspberries, making raspberry wine is one way to save the essence of this delectable fruit — and maybe even to share the wealth.

YIELD: 1 GALLON (3.8 L)

2½ pounds (1.14 kg) raspberries

1 Campden tablet (optional)

2½ pounds (1.14 kg) sugar

1 cup (240 ml) red grape juice concentrate

1 package (5–7 g) wine yeast

1 teaspoon (5 g) yeast nutrient

1½ cups (360 ml) orange juice, at room temperature

1 teaspoon (5 g) pectic enzyme

1 teaspoon (5 g) acid blend

1. Put the berries into a 2-gallon (7.6 L) plastic bucket or wastebasket, and pour 2 quarts (1.9 L) of boiling water over them. When they have cooled to warm, make a pulp with your hands. Add a Campden tablet, if desired, and let the mixture sit, covered with plastic wrap or foil, for four days. Stir daily; then strain the mixture through cheesecloth and add the sugar and grape juice concentrate. Stir the mixture until the sugar is dissolved.

2. In a jar, make a yeast starter culture by combining the wine yeast, yeast nutrient, and orange juice. Cover, shake vigorously, and let stand 1 to 3 hours, until bubbly; then add to the must.

3. Add the remaining ingredients and enough water to make 1 gallon (3.8 L) and pour the liquid into an airlocked fermentation vessel. When the fermentation is complete and the wine is clear, rack the wine into bottles and cork.

4. You will need to age this wine for at least three months for the best flavor — and you may never find a wait more difficult. Raspberry wines are so pretty and have such a delicious bouquet that waiting to sample them is the hardest part of the process.

Sweet Red Raspberry Wine

Raspberries are fragile fruits, but their flavors are robust. The finished wine made from red raspberries will be clear red; if you would like a golden raspberry wine, use one of the golden varieties. Be sure to use only ripe berries; only a few green or partly green berries can change the flavor of the finished wine.

YIELD: 1 GALLON (3.8 L)

4 pounds (1.8 kg) red raspberries

4 ounces (120 g) light raisins

1 Campden tablet (optional)

1 package (5–7 g) wine yeast

1 teaspoon (5 g) yeast nutrient

1½ cups (360 ml) orange juice, at room temperature

4 pounds (1.8 kg) sugar

1 teaspoon (5 g) acid blend

1. Crush the berries in a large, unchipped enamel or stainless steel container. Add the raisins and 2 quarts (1.9 L) of water. Add a Campden tablet, if desired. If you do so, let the mixture sit, well covered, for 24 hours, stirring two or three times before proceeding.

2. In a jar, make a yeast starter culture by combining the wine yeast, yeast nutrient, and orange juice. Cover, shake vigorously, and let stand 1 to 3 hours, until bubbly; then add to the must.

3. Strain the juice into a 2-gallon (7.6 L) plastic bucket or wastebasket (discard the pulp), and add half the sugar, the acid blend, and enough water to make 1 gallon (3.8 L). Allow the mixture to ferment for five days. Rack, add the remaining sugar, and ferment for 10 more days. Rack the wine into an air-locked fermentation vessel, and let it complete the fermentation process. When the wine is clear and no longer bubbling, rack into bottles; then cork and cellar the wine.

4. Wait at least six months before opening your first bottle.

Wild Black Raspberry Wine

This wine is all the more special because it's made from "found" bounty — those delectable wild raspberries that grow along fencerows and ditches. But poison ivy loves the same locations, so beware when you harvest wild raspberries. The delicate, dessert-quality flavor of black raspberry wine depends on the ripeness of the berries, and even a few green or partly green berries can affect the final flavor. Make sure your berries are completely ripe — even slightly overripe — for best results.

YIELD: 1 GALLON (3.8 L)

> 4 pounds (1.8 kg) wild black raspberries
>
> 8 ounces (240 g) raisins
>
> 1 Campden tablet (optional)
>
> 1 package (5–7 g) wine yeast
>
> 1 teaspoon (5 g) yeast nutrient
>
> 1½ cups (360 ml) orange juice, at room temperature
>
> 3½ pounds (1.6 kg) sugar
>
> 1 teaspoon (5 g) acid blend

1. In a large, unchipped enamel or stainless steel container, crush the berries; then add the raisins and 2 quarts (1.9 L) of water. Add a Campden tablet, if desired. If you do so, let the mixture sit for 24 hours, well covered, stirring two or three times before proceeding.

2. In a jar, make a yeast starter culture by combining the wine yeast, yeast nutrient, and orange juice. Cover, shake vigorously, and let stand 1 to 3 hours, until bubbly; then add to the must.

3. Strain the juice into a 2-gallon (7.6 L) plastic bucket or wastebasket (discard the pulp), and add half the sugar, the acid blend, and enough water to make 1 gallon (3.8 L). Allow the mixture to ferment for five days. Rack and add the remaining sugar, and ferment for 10 more days. Rack the wine into an air-locked fermentation vessel, and let it complete the fermentation process. When the wine is clear and no longer bubbling, rack into bottles; then cork and cellar the wine.

4. Wait at least six months before opening your first bottle.

Dry Rhubarb Wine

Pioneers once called rhubarb "pie plant" because it was usually the first "fruit" available in springtime for making eagerly anticipated pies after fruitless winters. Today, we use rhubarb for a variety of homemade wines because it is abundant and tasty. Here is a recipe for a dry table wine using the tangy pie plant.

YIELD: 1 GALLON (3.8 L)

3 pounds (1.4 kg) rhubarb stalks, sliced into ½-inch pieces

8 ounces (240 g) golden raisins, chopped

2½ pounds (1.14 kg) white sugar

¼ teaspoon (1.25 g) tannin

1 teaspoon (5 g) pectic enzyme

1 Campden tablet (optional)

1 teaspoon (5 g) orange zest

1 package (5–7 g) wine yeast

1 teaspoon (5 g) yeast nutrient

Juice of 1 orange

Additional orange juice, if necessary

1. Put the rhubarb and raisins in a fermentation vessel that can be fitted with an airlock. In a medium saucepan, bring ½ gallon (1.9 L) of water to a boil and add the sugar. Once the sugar is dissolved, pour the water over the mixture in the fermentation vessel. When the mixture is cool, add the tannin, pectic enzyme, Campden tablet (if desired), and zest. Let stand for 24 hours.

2. In a jar, make a yeast starter culture by combining the wine yeast, yeast nutrient, and orange juice. Cover, shake vigorously, and let stand 1 to 3 hours, until bubbly; then add to the must.

3. Ferment for two weeks; then rack off the solids. Top off with additional orange juice, if necessary, and let ferment for six more weeks. Rack again and ferment for one month. Rack, bottle, and cellar the wine.

4. Wait six months before sampling.

Choose vibrant red stalks of rhubarb for a colorful wine; select greener stalks if you prefer a white wine. Although the color is affected, there will be no real impact on the taste.

Strawberry-Rhubarb Wine

This recipe is for a fairly dry wine. To make it into an interesting dessert wine, you can sweeten it to taste and add potassium sorbate to keep the wine from refermenting.

YIELD: 1 GALLON (3.8 L)

2 pounds (900 g) red rhubarb stalks

2 pounds (900 g) ripe strawberries

1 pound (450 g) sugar

1 pound (450 g) honey

1 teaspoon (5 g) orange zest

12 ounces (360 ml) preservative-free apple juice concentrate

¼ teaspoon (1.25 g) tannin

1 teaspoon (5 g) yeast nutrient

1 teaspoon (5 g) pectic enzyme

1 Campden tablet (optional)

1 package (5–7 g) wine yeast

Juice of 2 oranges

1. Cut the rhubarb into ½-inch pieces. In a bowl, crush the strawberries, and then transfer the berries and rhubarb to a fermentation vessel fitted with an airlock. In a medium saucepan, boil the sugar and honey in ½ gallon (1.9 L) of water, skimming off the foam. When no more foam rises to the top, add the orange zest and apple juice concentrate. Pour the mixture over the fruits in the fermentation vessel. Add the tannin, yeast nutrient, pectic enzyme, and Campden tablet (if desired), and let stand for 24 hours.

2. Add the wine yeast to the mixture and ferment for two weeks. Rack off the solids, top off with the orange juice, and let ferment for six more weeks. Rack again and ferment one more month. Rack one last time, and then bottle and cellar the wine.

3. Wait six months before sampling.

Rose Hip Wine

Because roses and apples are different branches on the same family tree, you'll find that rose hip wine has a flavor reminiscent of apple wine, but more delicate. Like apples, rose hips need to be ripe before they taste sweet and mellow, so use only deep orange to bright red rose hips. Wash the rose hips thoroughly, and be sure to know their source. Rose hips from bushes that have been treated with a systemic insecticide will contain traces of pesticide. For best flavor, gather rose hips from hedgerows in the fall after the first frost.

YIELD: 1 GALLON (3.8 L)

1½ pounds (675 g) fresh rose hips *or* ½ pound (225 g) dried rose hips

2¼ pounds (1 kg) sugar

1 Campden tablet (optional)

1 package (5–7 g) wine yeast

1 teaspoon (5 g) yeast nutrient

1½ cups (360 ml) orange juice, at room temperature

1 teaspoon (5 g) citric acid *or* the juice of 1 lemon

1 teaspoon (5 g) pectic enzyme

1. Wash the rose hips, cut them in half, and crush them in a 2-gallon (7.6 L) plastic container. Add the sugar; then pour 2 quarts (1.9 L) of water over the mixture. Add a Campden tablet, if desired, and let sit, covered, for 24 hours.

2. In a jar, make a yeast starter culture by combining the wine yeast, yeast nutrient, and orange juice. Cover, shake vigorously, and let stand 1 to 3 hours, until bubbly; then add to the must.

3. Add the rest of the ingredients. Let the mixture stand for one week, stirring daily. Strain out the solids, and add enough water to make 1 gallon (3.8 L). Pour the liquid into an airlocked fermentation vessel, and let stand for three months. Rack the mixture and let it ferment to completion, racking as often as necessary to ensure a fine, clear wine. (You'll be able to tell if your wine needs additional racking if you notice a layer of sediment on the bottom of the container.) When fermentation is complete, bottle, cork, and cellar the wine.

4. Wait at least two or three months before you sample.

Sweet Wild Strawberry Dessert Wine

A fine finale to any meal — lovely served with fresh fruit and cheese.

YIELD: 1 GALLON (3.8 L)

4 pounds (1.8 kg) wild strawberries

4 ounces (120 g) white raisins

1 Campden tablet (optional)

1 package (5–7 g) wine yeast

1 teaspoon (5 g) yeast nutrient

1½ cups (360 ml) orange juice, at room temperature

1 teaspoon (5 g) acid blend

4 pounds (1.8 kg) sugar

1. Wash and hull the berries. Put them into a 2-gallon (7.6 L) plastic bucket or wastebasket and crush. Add the raisins and 2 quarts (1.9 L) of water. Add a Campden tablet, if desired, to kill off any wild yeasts that are present on the berries. Let the mixture stand, well covered, for 24 hours, stirring two or three times at intervals. Strain through cheesecloth and discard the solids.

2. In a jar, make a yeast starter culture by combining the wine yeast, yeast nutrient, and orange juice. Cover, shake vigorously, and let stand 1 to 3 hours, until bubbly; then add to the must.

3. Add the acid blend and half of the sugar, and let the mixture ferment for one week. Add the rest of the sugar and enough water to make 1 gallon (3.8 L), and ferment the mixture in an airlocked fermentation vessel for 10 days. Rack into another airlocked vessel, and let the mixture ferment to completion; then bottle, cork, and cellar the wine.

4. Wait at least six months before opening a bottle.

VARIATION: It's the Berries Wine
Substitute red raspberries for half the strawberries in this recipe.

Strawberry Wine

Our first strawberry wines were a surprise. We expected something sweet and syrupy — a little like the juice that soaks into strawberry shortcake. Instead, though, we tasted a crisp, deliciously sophisticated wine.

YIELD: 1 GALLON (3.8 L)

3 pounds (1.4 kg) strawberries

2½ pounds (1.14 kg) sugar

1 Campden tablet (optional)

1 package (5–7 g) wine yeast

1 teaspoon (5 g) yeast nutrient

1½ cups (360 ml) orange juice, at room temperature

1 teaspoon (5 g) citric acid *or* the juice of 1 lemon

½ teaspoon (2.5 g) grape tannin *or* 1 tablespoon (15 ml) strong tea

1. Wash and hull the berries, and put them into a 2-gallon (7.6 L) plastic bucket or wastebasket. Mash the sugar into the berries, and add 2 quarts (1.9 L) of water. Add the Campden tablet, if desired, and let the mixture stand, well covered, for 24 hours, stirring two or three times at intervals. Pour the mixture into a large glass or plastic container, and add enough water to make 1 gallon (3.8 L). Strain out the solids and discard them.

2. In a jar, make a yeast starter culture by combining the wine yeast, yeast nutrient, and orange juice. Cover, shake vigorously, and let stand 1 to 3 hours, until bubbly; then add to the must.

3. Add the citric acid and the tannin, and pour the mixture into a 1-gallon (3.8 L) airlocked fermentation vessel. Allow the mixture to ferment to completion, racking as needed for clarity. When it has finished fermenting, bottle, cork, and cellar the wine.

4. Wait at least six months before sampling.

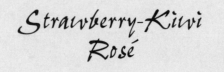

Strawberry-Kiwi Rosé

This wine will be a bit lighter in color than one made only from strawberries. But the flavors of the berries and the kiwi are quite similar, so the combination is a tantalizing blend that tastes mostly, but not entirely, like strawberries. It's a delicious difference.

YIELD: 1 GALLON (3.8 L)

2 pounds (900 g) kiwifruit, peeled and chopped

2 pounds (900 g) fresh strawberries, hulled and chopped

2½ pounds (1.14 kg) white sugar

Juice of 1 lemon

Juice of 1 orange

1 teaspoon (5 g) orange zest

¼ teaspoon (1.25 g) tannin

1 teaspoon (5 g) yeast nutrient

1 teaspoon (5 g) pectic enzyme

1 Campden tablet (optional)

1 package (5–7 g) wine yeast

1. Put the kiwi and strawberries into a 2-gallon (7.6 L) plastic bucket, wastebasket, or other fermentation vessel. In a medium saucepan, boil ½ gallon (1.9 L) of water and add the sugar. Pour the sugar water over the fruit. Add the lemon juice, orange juice, orange zest, tannin, yeast nutrient, pectic enzyme, and the Campden tablet (if desired). Let stand, covered, for 24 hours.

2. Add the yeast and let the mixture ferment for one week, stirring daily. Remove the solids. Pour the liquid into an airlocked fermentation vessel, and let ferment for one month. Rack again and let ferment for two months. Rack again; then bottle, cork, and cellar the wine.

3. Wait at least six months before you open your first bottle.

Chapter Three

MAKING WINES FROM FLOWERS, NUTS & VEGETABLES

Whe you make wines from flowers, nuts, and vegetables and serve them to your guests, you'll be treating them to an experience that they're unlikely to have at anyone else's table. As with fruit wines, the ingredients you use to make wines from flowers, nuts, and vegetables should be fresh, flavorful, and unblemished. Because flowers are not generally considered a food source, be sure that you know what plant you are using, where it came from, and whether the flower has been exposed to insecticides, particularly systemic ones.

Nuts, in particular, need to be tasted before you use them in wine. Nuts have a high oil content and may therefore taste rancid without looking spoiled. Discard nuts that are shriveled, discolored, or otherwise suspect. Low-oil-content nuts, like almonds, make the best wines.

Vegetables do not generally have these problems, and some of them make surprisingly good wines. Among our favorites are those made from carrot and parsnip, but we've also had success with potato wines.

Almond Wine

A little like a mild amaretto, almond wine is wonderful with desserts: Try it with pound cake and cream-filled pastries. But it's equally good with fruit tarts — especially cherry, a fruit that complements the nutty wine to perfection.

YIELD: 1 GALLON (3.8 L)

1½ ounces (45 g) almonds

1 pound (450 g) light raisins

1 cup (240 ml) grape juice concentrate

2¼ pounds (1 kg) sugar

Juice of 2 lemons

1 teaspoon (5 g) lemon zest

1 Campden tablet (optional)

1 package (5–7 g) wine yeast

1 teaspoon (5 g) yeast nutrient

1½ cups (120 ml) orange juice, at room temperature

1 teaspoon (5 g) pectic enzyme

1. Mince the almonds and raisins in a food processor. Transfer the nuts and raisins to a large, unchipped enamel or stainless steel pot, and add enough water to cover. Simmer gently for about 1 hour, making sure to keep enough water in the pan to prevent scorching. Strain the liquid into a 2-gallon (7.6 L) plastic bucket or wastebasket, and discard the solids. Add the grape juice concentrate and enough water to make 1 gallon (3.8 L). Add the sugar, lemon juice, and lemon zest. Add a Campden tablet, if desired, and let sit, well covered, for 24 hours.

2. In a jar, make a yeast starter culture by combining the wine yeast, yeast nutrient, and orange juice. Cover, shake vigorously, and let stand 1 to 3 hours, until bubbly; then add to the must.

3. Add the pectic enzyme and cover loosely. Allow the mixture to ferment for about 10 days. Rack it to an airlocked fermentation vessel, and let the wine ferment to completion, racking as necessary to clear the wine. Bottle, cork, and cellar the wine.

4. This wine is best if you wait three months before sampling.

Red Beet Wine

If you just pour this wine and don't tell people what it's made from, they may think they're tasting a particularly interesting Burgundy. The color is rich and red, and the wine retains just a hint of the earthy flavor to give it a unique character. You can get something of the same flavor in a lighter hue by using golden beets instead of red ones.

YIELD: 1 GALLON (3.8 L)

3 pounds (1.4 kg) beets, greens removed

12 ounces (360 ml) orange juice concentrate

2 pounds (900 g) white sugar

1 pound (450 g) honey

2 teaspoons (10 g) fresh orange zest

1 Campden tablet (optional)

1 package (5–7 g) Montrachet wine yeast

1 teaspoon (5 g) pectic enzyme

1 teaspoon (5 g) yeast nutrient

1½ cups (360 ml) orange juice, at room temperature

¼ teaspoon (1.25 g) tannin

1. Wash the beets and place them in a large pot with enough water to cover. Simmer over low heat until the beets are tender. Remove the vegetables from the liquid, reserving a cup of the beets for later use. Add the orange juice concentrate, sugar, and honey to the liquid, bring to a boil, and then simmer for 10 minutes, removing and discarding any scum. Remove from the heat.

2. Crush the reserved beets into a coarse paste, and stir them back into the liquid. Add the orange zest. Transfer the mixture to a 2-gallon (7.6 L) plastic wastebasket or bucket. Add cool water to bring the volume up to about 1 gallon (3.8 L). Add a Campden tablet, if desired, and let the mixture sit, loosely covered, for 24 hours.

3. In a jar, make a yeast starter culture by combining the wine yeast, pectic enzyme, yeast nutrient, and orange juice. Cover, shake vigorously, and let stand 1 to 3 hours, until bubbly; then add to the must.

4. Add the tannin and rack into a 1-gallon (3.8 L) airlocked fermentation vessel. Let the mixture ferment for three to four months, racking as needed to clear; then bottle, cork, and cellar the wine.

5. Wait six months before sampling.

Spiced Beet Wine

Do you like your beets ho-hum or Harvard? Your preference in table beets will give a hint as to whether you'd prefer natural beet wine or the hardier spiced variety. Both have deep color, but the spiced beets are more complex and sophisticated.

YIELD: 1 GALLON (3.8 L)

3 pounds (1.4 kg) beets, greens removed

12 ounces (360 ml) orange juice concentrate

2 pounds (900 g) white sugar

1 pound (450 g) honey

1 cinnamon stick

1 allspice berry

¼ teaspoon (1.25 g) ground nutmeg

2 teaspoons (10 g) fresh orange zest

1 Campden tablet (optional)

1 package (5–7 g) Montrachet wine yeast

1 teaspoon (5 g) pectic enzyme

1 teaspoon (5 g) yeast nutrient

1½ cups (360 ml) orange juice, at room temperature

¼ teaspoon (1.25 g) tannin

1. Wash the beets and place them in a large pot. Cover with water. Simmer over low heat until the beets are tender. Remove the vegetables from the liquid, reserving a cup of beets for later use. Add the orange juice concentrate, sugar, honey, and spices to the liquid. Bring the mixture to a boil, and then simmer for 10 minutes, removing and discarding any scum. Remove from the heat.

2. Crush the reserved beets into a coarse paste and stir them back into the liquid. Add the orange zest, and transfer the mixture to a 2-gallon (7.6 L) plastic wastebasket or bucket. Add cool water to bring the volume up to about 1 gallon (3.8 L). Add the Campden tablet, if desired, and let the mixture sit, loosely covered, for 24 hours.

3. In a jar, make a yeast starter culture by combining the wine yeast, pectic enzyme, yeast nutrient, and orange juice. Cover, shake vigorously, and let stand 1 to 3 hours, until bubbly; then add to the must.

4. Add the tannin and rack into a 1-gallon (3.8 L) airlocked fermentation vessel. Let the mixture ferment for three to four months, racking as needed to clear. Bottle, cork, and cellar the wine.

5. Wait six months before sampling.

Carrot Wine

Carrots make a delicious wine because they are quite sweet. The finished wine is golden and very mellow. Take great care that the wine is clear; golden wines must sparkle when they are served to avoid looking artificial.

YIELD: 1 GALLON (3.8 L)

6 pounds (2.7 kg) carrots, scrubbed and sliced

12 ounces (360 ml) orange juice concentrate

8 ounces (240 g) golden raisins, chopped

2 pounds (900 g) white sugar

1 pound (450 g) clover honey

1 Campden tablet (optional)

1 package (5–7 g) Montrachet wine yeast

1 teaspoon (5 g) pectic enzyme

1 teaspoon (5 g) yeast nutrient

1½ cups (360 ml) orange juice, at room temperature

1. Place the carrots in a large pot with 2 quarts (1.9 L) of water. Add the orange juice concentrate, raisins, sugar, and honey, and boil for 10 minutes, removing any scum that rises to the surface. Cool. Strain out the carrots, reserving 1 cup. Crush the carrots into a paste and add them back to the liquid. Transfer the mixture to a 2-gallon (7.6 L) plastic bucket or wastebasket. Add 2 quarts (1.9 L) of water. Add the Campden tablet, if desired, and let sit, well covered, for 24 hours.

2. In a jar, make a starter culture by combining the wine yeast, pectic enzyme, yeast nutrient, and the 1½ cups (360 ml) of orange juice. Cover, shake vigorously, and let stand 1 to 3 hours, until bubbly; then add to the must.

3. Rack into a 1-gallon (3.8 L) airlocked fermentation vessel. Let the mixture ferment for three to four months, racking as needed to clear. Bottle, cork, and cellar the wine.

4. Wait six months before sampling.

Clove Wine

Clove wine may not be for everyone, but we like to make a batch or two about midsummer so it will be ready for the dozens of uses we find for it during the holiday season — starting with Halloween and continuing right up until the end of the year. It's a delightful addition to mulled wine and cider and gives a distinctively different taste to eggnog and sangria. But our favorite use for clove wine is for soaking the cheesecloths that will cover our holiday fruitcakes — yum! And, of course, you can drink it — alone or as a refreshing addition to orange-garnished iced tea.

YIELD: 1 GALLON (3.8 L)

1 ounce (30 g) whole cloves

2¼ pounds (1 kg) brown sugar

6 ounces (180 ml) tangerine juice concentrate

1 Campden tablet (optional)

1 package (5–7 g) wine yeast

1 teaspoon (5 g) yeast nutrient

1½ cups (360 ml) orange juice, at room temperature

1 teaspoon (5 g) pectic enzyme

1. Tie the cloves into a coffee filter and, in a medium saucepan, simmer for about 1 hour in enough water to cover. Put the sugar in a 2-gallon (7.6 L) plastic container, and add the clove liquor and 2 quarts (1.9 L) of boiling water. Add the tangerine juice concentrate. Add the Campden tablet, if desired, and let sit, well covered, for 24 hours.

2. In a jar, make a yeast starter culture by combining the wine yeast, yeast nutrient, and orange juice. Cover, shake vigorously, and let stand 1 to 3 hours, until bubbly; then add to the must.

3. Add the pectic enzyme, cover loosely, and allow the mixture to ferment for about 10 days. Rack to an airlocked fermentation vessel, and let the wine ferment to completion, racking as necessary to clear it. Bottle, cork, and cellar the wine.

4. This wine is best if you wait three months before sampling.

Clove-Ginger Wine

Wonderful wine coolers result from mixing this wine with lemon-lime soda or a tall glass of iced tea. But we like it best as a marinade for chicken that's to be seared in a wok or served sizzling from the grill. And if you like a little more spice to your fruitcake, use clove-ginger wine for soaking.

YIELD: 1 GALLON (3.8 L)

3 lemons

1 orange

1 ounce (30 g) gingerroot

1 ounce (30 g) whole cloves

2¼ pounds (1 kg) light brown sugar

1 Campden tablet (optional)

1 package (5–7 g) wine yeast

1 teaspoon (5 g) yeast nutrient

1½ cups (360 ml) orange juice, at room temperature

1 teaspoon (5 g) pectic enzyme

1. Grate the lemon and orange rind (avoiding the white inner rind), and place the grated rind in a small muslin bag. Bruise the ginger and cloves and add them to the bag. (Or use a coffee filter to hold these ingredients and tie it shut with strong thread.) Juice the lemons and the orange and set the juice aside. Place the muslin bag and 2 quarts (1.9 L) of boiling water in a nonaluminum saucepan; simmer for 1 hour. Put the sugar into a 2-gallon (7.6 L) plastic container and pour the water over it. Add the juices from the lemons and orange. Add a Campden tablet, if desired, and let sit, covered, for 24 hours.

2. In a jar, make a yeast starter culture by combining the wine yeast, yeast nutrient, and the 1½ cups of orange juice. Cover, shake vigorously, and let stand 1 to 3 hours, until bubbly; then add to the must.

3. Add the pectic enzyme and enough water to make 1 gallon (3.8 L). Allow the mixture to stand, loosely covered, for four days. Rack into an airlocked fermentation vessel and let it ferment, racking as necessary to clear the wine. When the fermentation is complete, bottle, cork, and cellar the wine.

4. Wait at least six months before sampling.

Red Clover Wine

In South Dakota, where prairie flowers still tuck themselves into nooks and crannies of the hayfields, red clover is found bounty to farm kids. They plucked the tubular little petals from the flower head and tasted the sweet nectar at the base. Red clover wine has some of that same charm. The clover heads will not impart too much color to the wine; the red refers to the color of the clover, not to the color of the wine.

YIELD: 1 GALLON (3.8 L)

1 gallon (3.8 L) clover heads

3 pounds (1.4 kg) sugar

8 ounces (240 g) light raisins

1 Campden tablet (optional)

1 teaspoon (5 g) acid blend

1 package (5–7 g) wine yeast

1 teaspoon (5 g) pectic enzyme

1 teaspoon (5 g) yeast nutrient

1½ cups (360 ml) orange juice, at room temperature

1. Remove the stems and the base from the clover heads. Place the petals in an enamel or stainless steel pot with 1 gallon (3.8 L) of water, and bring the mixture to a boil. Remove from the heat and add half the sugar and the raisins. Cool. Add a Campden tablet, if desired, and let the mixture sit, well covered, for 24 hours. Transfer the mixture to a 2-gallon (7.6 L) plastic container and add the acid blend.

2. In a jar, make a yeast starter culture by combining the wine yeast, pectic enzyme, yeast nutrient, and orange juice. Cover, shake vigorously, and let stand 1 to 3 hours, until bubbly; then add to the must.

3. Allow the mixture to sit, loosely covered, for five days. Add the rest of the sugar, cover again, and wait another seven days. Rack into an airlocked fermentation vessel and wait another five days. If the fermentation is complete at this time and the wine has cleared, you may bottle and loosely cork the wine. If you don't get any cork-popping within several days, force the corks completely into the bottles and cellar the wine.

4. Wait at least six months before sampling.

White Clover Wine

This wine is white and wonderfully delicate. It may be a bit drier than the red clover wine, as white clover seems to have a little less sweetness. White clover may be more readily available, though.

YIELD: 1 GALLON (3.8 L)

1 gallon (3.8 L) clover heads

8 ounces (240 g) light raisins, chopped

3 pounds (1.4 kg) sugar

1 Campden tablet (optional)

1 package (5–7 g) wine yeast

1 teaspoon (5 g) pectic enzyme

1 teaspoon (5 g) yeast nutrient

1½ cups (360 ml) orange juice, at room temperature

1 ounce (30 g) citric acid

1. Pull out the petals from the clover heads and discard the base of the flowers. Put the petals in a large, stainless steel or enamel pot with 3½ quarts (3.3 L) of water, and bring the mixture to a boil. Remove from the heat and add half the sugar. Add the chopped raisins. Cool. Add a Campden tablet, if desired, and let sit, well covered, for 24 hours.

2. In a jar, make a yeast starter culture by combining the wine yeast, pectic enzyme, yeast nutrient, and orange juice. Cover, shake vigorously, and let stand 1 to 3 hours, until bubbly; then add to the must.

3. Add the citric acid and transfer the mixture to a 2-gallon (7.6 L) plastic container. Let ferment for five days, loosely covered. Add the rest of the sugar and stir until it is dissolved. Rack and ferment the liquid for 10 more days. Rack into a 1-gallon (3.8 L) airlocked fermentation vessel and allow the wine to ferment to completion. When fermentation is finished, bottle, cork and cellar the wine.

4. Wait six months before sampling.

Cornmeal Wine

Cornmeal wine is initially a bit slower to ferment than many other wines, so be patient with it. Once the fermentation gets going, it makes a good, dry wine.

YIELD: 1 GALLON (3.8 L)

2 lemons

3 oranges

1½ pounds (675 g) cornmeal

2¼ pounds (1 kg) sugar

3 pints (1.5 L) grape juice concentrate

¼ ounce (about 7 g) ground rice (use a food processor or blender)

1 Campden tablet (optional)

1 package (5–7 g) wine yeast

1 teaspoon (5 g) yeast nutrient

1½ cups (360 ml) orange juice, at room temperature

1 teaspoon (5 g) pectic enzyme

1. Grate the outer rinds of the oranges and lemons; discard the solids and the white inner rind. Squeeze the juice from the oranges and lemons into a 2-gallon (7.6 L) plastic container. Add the grated rind to the container, along with the cornmeal, sugar, grape juice concentrate, and rice. Add enough water to make 1 gallon (3.8 L). Add a Campden tablet, if desired, and let the mixture sit, well covered, for 24 hours.

2. In a jar, make a yeast starter culture by combining the wine yeast, yeast nutrient, and 1½ cups (360 ml) of orange juice. Cover, shake vigorously, and let stand 1 to 3 hours, until bubbly; then add to the must.

3. Add the pectic enzyme. Let the mixture sit for 30 days, loosely covered. Strain out the solids, transfer the liquid to a 1-gallon (3.8 L) airlocked fermentation vessel, and allow it to ferment for 30 days. When fermentation is complete, bottle the wine, cork it, and store in a cool cellar.

4. Wait at least six months before opening the first bottle.

Dandelion Wine

Country folks had an optimistic and ecologically sound solution to dandelion problems — they made dandelion wine. Once you've tried a little of this golden nectar, you'll know why author Ray Bradbury called it "bottled sunshine." The key to making delicious dandelion wine is using clean, chemical-free petals — and only petals. The green stuff that surrounds the dandelion flower will give your wine an off-flavor, so be sure to peel it back and then pull or cut the petals from the stems. Dandelion wine has such a delicate flavor that we prefer to use acid blend rather than lemon juice to avoid too much citrus taste.

YIELD: 1 GALLON (3.8 L)

6 cups (1.5 L) dandelion petals

2 pounds (900 g) granulated sugar

1 pound (450 g) light raisins

1 tablepoon (15 g) acid blend

1 Campden tablet (optional)

1 package (5–7 g) wine yeast

1 teaspoon (5 g) yeast nutrient

1½ cups (360 ml) orange juice, at room temperature

1 teaspoon (5 g) pectic enzyme

1. Wash and prepare the dandelion petals. Place them and the sugar, raisins, and acid blend in a 2-gallon (7.6 L) plastic wastebasket or bucket. Bring 1 gallon (3.8 L) of water to a boil and pour it into the mixture. Add a Campden tablet, if desired, and let the mixture sit for 24 hours. Otherwise, proceed as follows. Cool the mixture to lukewarm.

2. In a jar, make a yeast starter culture by combining the wine yeast, yeast nutrient, and orange juice. Cover, shake vigorously, and let stand 1 to 3 hours, until bubbly; then add to the must.

3. Add the pectic enzyme, and ferment for three days in the original container, loosely covered with plastic wrap or foil. Then rack the liquid into a 2-gallon (7.6 L) airlocked fermentation vessel, and allow it to ferment to completion — about three months. Rack again; then bottle, cork, and cellar the wine.

4. Wait at least six months before sampling.

Elderflower Wine I

If you just can't wait for the elderberries, try elderflowers instead! Like most flower wines, elderflower wine is delicate in flavor and light in color. It has an elusive bouquet and undertones of citrus.

YIELD: 1 GALLON (3.8 L)

> 1 lemon
>
> 1 pint (450 g) fresh elderflower heads (tightly packed)
>
> 1 Campden tablet (optional)
>
> 3 pounds (1.4 kg) granulated sugar
>
> 1 package (5–7 g) wine yeast
>
> 1 teaspoon (5 g) yeast nutrient
>
> 1½ cups (360 ml) orange juice
>
> 1 teaspoon (5 g) pectic enzyme

1. Grate the lemon rind (avoiding the white inner rind), and stir it and the elderflowers into a 2-gallon (7.6 L) glass or plastic container. (Wash the elderflowers thoroughly before using, however, especially if they grow near a road.) Bring 1 gallon (3.8 L) of water to a boil and pour it over the elderflower mixture. Add a Campden tablet, if desired, and let sit, well covered, for three days.

2. Pour the mixture over the sugar in a large stainless steel or enamel container. Bring to a boil, remove from the heat, and let cool to lukewarm. Strain the mixture into an airlocked fermentation vessel. Squeeze the juice out of the lemon and add it to the mixture.

3. In a jar, make a yeast starter culture by combining the wine yeast, yeast nutrient, and orange juice. Cover, shake vigorously, and let stand 1 to 3 hours, until bubbly; then add to the must.

4. Add the pectic enzyme and let the fermentation proceed to completion (about four months), racking as necessary to clear the wine.

5. Wait at least six months before opening your first bottle.

Elderflower Wine II

Because this wine has a grape component, it will have a more vinous character than the preceding elderflower wine, but it will still have the fine white color that is a trait of many flower wines. If you are a fan of the grape, you may find this version very much to your liking. Be aware that the variety of grape used to make the raisins or the concentrate will affect the flavor of this wine.

YIELD: 1 GALLON (3.8 L)

1½ cups (360 g) fresh elder-flowers *or* ½ ounce (15 g) dried flowers

3 lemons

½ pound (225 g) raisins *or* ½ cup (120 ml) white grape concentrate

1 Campden tablet (optional)

2¾ pounds (1.25 kg) sugar

1 teaspoon (5 g) grape tannin

1 package (5–7 g) wine yeast

1 teaspoon (5 g) yeast nutrient

1½ cups (360 ml) orange juice, at room temperature

1 teaspoon (5 g) pectic enzyme

1. Cut the washed elderflowers from their stems with scissors. Grate the lemon rind (avoiding the white inner rind). Reserve the lemons. Mix the grated rind with the elderflowers in a large enamel or stainless steel pot, and pour 2 quarts (1.9 L) of boiling water over them. Let cool. Add the raisins and a Campden tablet, if desired, and let the mixture sit, loosely covered with plastic wrap or foil, for three days.

2. Add the sugar and bring the mixture to a boil. Lower the heat and simmer for 5 to 6 minutes. Let the mixture cool, and strain it into a 2-gallon (7.6 L) plastic container. Juice the lemons, and then add the lemon juice and tannin to the mixture.

3. In a jar, make a yeast starter culture by combining the wine yeast, yeast nutrient, and orange juice. Cover, shake vigorously, and let stand 1 to 3 hours, until bubbly; then add to the must.

4. Add the pectic enzyme and let stand until the mixture is clear. Rack the mixture into an airlocked fermentation vessel, and let stand for about two months. Rack again, and bottle when the fermentation is complete.

5. Wait at least six months before sampling.

Garlic Wine

Because the garlic remains whole in this recipe, and part of it is caramelized, you won't get the harsh flavor associated with the chopped, raw herb. Combined with apple juice, the garlic will be mellow and mild. This is not a sipping wine. It is intended for the best wine-based salad dressings and marinades you've ever tasted!

YIELD: 1 GALLON (3.8 L)

12 large garlic bulbs

12 ounces (360 ml) apple juice concentrate

Juice of 1 lemon

2 teaspoons (10 g) lemon zest

1 Campden tablet (optional)

1 package (5–7 g) Montrachet wine yeast

1 teaspoon (5 g) pectic enzyme

1 teaspoon (5 g) yeast nutrient

1½ cups (360 ml) orange juice, at room temperature

¼ teaspoon (1.25 g) tannin

1. Divide garlic into two piles, one with 8 heads and the other with 4 heads. Separate and peel garlic cloves, discarding any with brown spots. Wrap the cloves from 4 garlic heads in a piece of aluminum foil and seal tightly. Bake in a 350°F (177°C) oven for 2 hours to caramelize the sugars.

2. Place the baked garlic and the cloves from the remaining 8 heads of garlic in a large pot with 2 quarts (1.9 L) of water. Boil for 45 minutes, replacing the evaporated water as needed. Strain out the cloves and return the garlic water to the pot. Add the apple juice concentrate and boil for 5 minutes. Remove from heat and stir in lemon juice and lemon zest. Let cool for 1 hour. Strain out the zest and transfer liquid to a 1-gallon (3.8 L) plastic bucket. Add a Campden tablet, if desired, and let the mixture sit, loosely covered, for 24 hours.

3. In a jar, make a yeast starter culture by combining the wine yeast, pectic enzyme, yeast nutrient, and orange juice. Cover, shake vigorously, and let stand 1 to 3 hours, until bubbly; then add to the must.

4. Add the tannin and let the mixture sit, loosely covered, for seven days. Rack into a 1-gallon (3.8 L) airlocked fermentation vessel, topping off with water if necessary. Let the mixture ferment for three to four months, racking as needed to clear. Bottle, cork, and cellar the wine.

5. Wait six months before using this wine to make wonderful meat marinades.

Dry Ginger Wine

Think of ginger ale with heady, tropical overtones and an adult flair. This white wine has the vinous quality imparted by the grape juice, the zip of ginger, and a subtle hint of banana that brings a charming balance to the finished wine.

YIELD: 1 GALLON (3.8 L)

3 ounces (85 g) whole gingerroot

1 cup (240 ml) white grape juice concentrate

1½ pounds (675 g) bananas

1 Campden tablet (optional)

1 package (5–7 g) wine yeast

1 teaspoon (5 g) pectic enzyme

1 teaspoon (5 g) yeast nutrient

1½ cups (360 ml) orange juice, at room temperature

2 pounds (900 g) sugar

1. Break the gingerroot into pieces, and mix the pieces with the grape juice concentrate in a 2-gallon (7.6 L) plastic container. Add 2 quarts (1.9 L) of boiling water. Peel the bananas and force them through a strainer; add to the ginger mixture and cool. Add the Campden tablet, if desired, and let stand, well covered, for 24 hours.

2. In a jar, make a yeast starter culture by combining the wine yeast, pectic enzyme, yeast nutrient, and orange juice. Cover, shake vigorously, and let stand 1 to 3 hours, until bubbly; then add to the must.

3. Add the sugar and enough water to make 1 gallon (3.8 L). Let the pulp ferment, loosely covered, for 10 days. Rack into an airlocked fermentation vessel, and let the mixture ferment for three months, racking as necessary to clear. When fermentation is complete, bottle, cork, and cellar the wine.

4. Wait at least six months before opening your first bottle.

VARIATION: Tropical Ginger Wine

Substitute brown sugar for white sugar in this recipe for a more intense flavor.

Honeysuckle Wine

Honeysuckle wine captures some elusive essence of spring. It's soft and subtle alone, and delectable in summer wine coolers. **Caution: Use only the blossoms of the vine; the berries are poisonous.**

YIELD: 1 GALLON (3.8 L)

4 cups (1 L) honeysuckle blossoms (lightly packed)

2¼ pounds (1 kg) sugar

½ cup (120 ml) white grape juice concentrate

2 teaspoons (10 g) acid blend

1 Campden tablet (optional)

1 package (5–7 g) wine yeast

1 teaspoon (5 g) pectic enzyme

1 teaspoon (5 g) yeast nutrient

1½ cups (360 ml) orange juice, at room temperature

1 teaspoon (5 g) tannin *or* 1 tablespoon (15 ml) strong tea

1. Wash the honeysuckle blossoms in a colander under cold water. In a 2-gallon (7.6 L) plastic container, mix the flowers, half the sugar, the grape juice concentrate, and the acid blend. Add enough water to make 1 gallon (3.8 L). Add a Campden tablet, if desired, and let the mixture sit for 24 hours.

2. In a jar, make a yeast starter culture by combining the wine yeast, pectic enzyme, yeast nutrient, and orange juice. Cover, shake vigorously, and let stand 1 to 3 hours, until bubbly; then add to the must.

3. Add the tannin and allow the mixture to ferment, loosely covered, for seven days. Rack the liquid into a 2-gallon (7.6 L) airlocked fermentation vessel, and let it ferment to completion, racking as necessary to clear the wine. When the fermentation is complete, bottle, cork, and cellar the wine.

4. Wait at least six months before sampling.

Marigold Wine

Don't let the smell of fresh-picked marigolds put you off. This lightly golden wine (the color may vary slightly, depending on how much burgundy and red are in the petals) has an interesting blend of flavors with undertones of citrus. For the whitest wines, use pale yellow or nearly white marigolds. Although you may use the dwarf, vividly colored varieties, we try to stick to the giant pale yellow varieties — they're easier to prepare and milder than those with more concentrated colors.

YIELD: 1 GALLON (3.8 L)

1 lemon

2 oranges

3½ quarts (3.3 L) marigold flowers (without the sepals and stems)

3 pounds (1.4 kg) sugar

1 Campden tablet (optional)

1 package (5–7 g) wine yeast

1 teaspoon (5 g) pectic enzyme

1 teaspoon (5 g) acid blend

1 teaspoon (5 g) yeast nutrient

1½ cups (360 ml) orange juice, at room temperature

1. Grate orange and lemon rinds. Reserve the fruit. Place rinds and flower petals in a 2-gallon (7.6 L) plastic container. Bring 1 gallon (3.8 L) of water to a boil, pour over the petal mixture, and add the sugar. Stir until the sugar dissolves. Add a Campden tablet, if desired, and let the mixture sit for 24 hours.

2. In a jar, make a yeast starter culture by combining the wine yeast, pectic enzyme, acid blend, yeast nutrient, and the 1½ cups (360 ml) of orange juice. Cover, shake vigorously, and let stand 1 to 3 hours, until bubbly. Add the starter culture to the must, and then add the juice of the lemon and oranges.

3. Let the mixture sit, loosely covered, for seven days. Strain out the solids and transfer the liquid to a 1-gallon (3.8 L) airlocked fermentation vessel. Allow the wine to ferment to completion — usually three to four weeks. Rack the wine and, if fermentation is complete, bottle, cork, and cellar it.

4. Wait at least six months before sampling the wine.

Parsnip Wine

Pattie once judged an amateur winemaking competition in Iowa that drew hundreds of contestants from several states. Because she had written about old-fashioned wines, the judges paired her with a well-known restaurateur to judge the "weird stuff." The restaurant owner poured some parsnip wine, swirled it in his glass, held it in front of the candle to judge its clarity, held it beneath his nose, and looked once again at the label before taking a timid sip. Then he turned to Pattie, tried a second sip, and said, "I think I'm in love."

YIELD: 1 GALLON (3.8 L)

6 pounds (2.7 kg) parsnips, well scrubbed

12 ounces (360 ml) apple juice concentrate

2½ pounds (1.14 kg) white sugar

1 Campden tablet (optional)

1 package (5–7 g) Montrachet wine yeast

1 teaspoon (5 g) pectic enzyme

1 teaspoon (5 g) yeast nutrient

1½ cups (360 ml) orange juice, at room temperature

Juice of 1 lemon

2 teaspoons (10 g) lemon zest

1. Put the parsnips in a large pot with 2 quarts (1.9 L) of water. Add the apple juice concentrate and sugar, and boil for 10 minutes, removing any scum from the surface. Let cool. Strain out the parsnips, reserving 1 cup (240 ml) of the vegetables. Crush the saved parsnips into a paste, and add to the liquid. Transfer the mixture into a 2-gallon (7.6 L) plastic bucket, and pour in 2 quarts (1.9 L) of water. Add a Campden tablet, if desired. Let sit, loosely covered, for 24 hours.

2. In a jar, make a yeast starter culture by combining the wine yeast, pectic enzyme, yeast nutrient, and orange juice. Cover, shake vigorously, and let stand 1 to 3 hours, until bubbly; then add to the must.

3. Add the lemon juice and zest. Rack into a 1-gallon (3.8 L) airlocked fermentation vessel, and let the mixture ferment for three to four months, racking as needed to clear. Bottle, cork, and cellar the wine.

4. Wait six months before sampling.

Pea Pod Wine

Snow peas straight from the vine seldom make it to the wok in our kitchens;
they're snack food all the way to the house. Pea pod wine retains some of that
can't-leave-it-alone character. The apple juice is mellow; the pea pod liquor is all
sweetness and light flavor. Don't tell your guests what's in this delicate, light-col-
ored wine: Make 'em guess.

YIELD: 1 GALLON (3.8 L)

4 pounds (1.8 kg) snow peas

1½ pounds (675 g) sugar

12 ounces (360 ml) apple juice concentrate

1 Campden tablet (optional)

1 package (5–7 g) Montrachet wine yeast

1 teaspoon (5 g) pectic enzyme

1 teaspoon (5 g) yeast nutrient

1½ cups (360 ml) orange juice, at room temperature

Juice of 1 lemon

2 teaspoons (10 g) fresh lemon zest

¼ teaspoon (1.25 g) tannin

1. Place the snow peas in a large pot with 2 quarts (1.9 L) of water, and simmer over low heat for 30 minutes. Remove the pods, and then dissolve the sugar and apple juice concentrate in the liquid. Transfer the mixture to a 2-gallon (7.6 L) plastic bucket or wastebasket, add 1 quart (about 1 L) of cold water, and let cool completely. Add a Campden tablet, if desired, and let the mixture sit, loosely covered, for 24 hours.

2. In a jar, make a yeast starter culture by combining the wine yeast, pectic enzyme, yeast nutrient, and orange juice. Cover, shake vigorously, and let stand 1 to 3 hours, until bubbly; then add to the must.

3. Add the lemon juice, lemon zest, and tannin. Rack into a 1-gallon (3.8 L) air-locked fermentation vessel. Let the mixture ferment for three to four months, racking as needed to clear. Bottle, cork, and cellar the wine.

4. Wait six months before sampling.

Potato Wine

In Kentucky and Tennessee, old-timers often tell of adding potatoes to their various wine recipes to increase the alcohol content and keeping qualities. This recipe makes a white wine that can be used in much the same way as vodka for a not-quite Virgin Mary or a simply smashing screwdriver. But because naturally fermented beverages don't have more than 18 percent alcohol, adding wine in the same proportion as you'd add vodka when you make these drinks results in a lighter, less alcoholic beverage.

YIELD: 1 GALLON (3.8 L)

3 pounds (1.4 kg) potatoes

4 pounds (1.8 kg) sugar

4 ounces (120 g) chopped light raisins

2 lemons

2 oranges

1 Campden tablet (optional)

1 package (5–7 g) wine yeast

1 teaspoon (5 g) pectic enzyme

1 teaspoon (5 g) yeast nutrient

1½ cups (360 ml) orange juice, at room temperature

1. Scrub the potatoes, but don't peel them. Cut them into quarters and cut away any bad spots or hollow centers. Grate them into a medium-size saucepan and add 3 quarts (2.8 L) of water. Bring to a boil and simmer for about 15 minutes, removing any scum that comes to the top. Continue to simmer until no more scum rises to the surface.

2. Put the sugar and the chopped raisins into a 2-gallon (7.6 L) plastic container, and strain the potato water onto them. Grate the outer rinds (avoiding the white inner rind) of the lemons and oranges, and juice them; add the grated rind and the juice to the container. Add a Campden tablet, if desired, and let the mixture sit, loosely covered, for 24 hours.

3. In a jar, make a yeast starter culture by combining the wine yeast, pectic enzyme, yeast nutrient, and the 1½ cups (360 ml) orange juice. Cover, shake vigorously, and let stand 1 to 3 hours, until bubbly; then add to the must.

4. Let the mixture sit, loosely covered, for seven days. Rack into a clean 2-gallon container, and let the mixture sit for 10 more days. Rack again, this time into a 1-gallon (3.8 L) airlocked fermentation vessel. Allow the wine to ferment to completion; then bottle, cork, and cellar it.

5. Wait six months before sampling.

Rose Petal Wine

We like to use red roses to make this wine so that the resulting liquid is pink and perfect — as delicate to look at as it is to drink. A word of caution about rose wines: Make sure that the rose petals you use come from bushes that haven't been treated with a systemic insecticide, and wash the petals carefully before you use them.

YIELD: 1 GALLON (3.8 L)

2 quarts (1.9 L) rose petals

2 pounds (900 g) sugar

1 cup (240 ml) white grape juice concentrate

1 Campden tablet (optional)

1 package (5–7 g) wine yeast

1 teaspoon (5 g) pectic enzyme

1 teaspoon (5 g) yeast nutrient

1½ cups (360 ml) orange juice, at room temperature

1 teaspoon (5 g) acid blend

1. Rinse the rose petals under cool running water. Bring 1 gallon (3.8 L) of water to a boil. Add the rose petals, sugar, and grape juice concentrate. Remove from the heat and let cool. Add a Campden tablet, if desired, and let sit, well covered, for 24 hours.

2. In a jar, make a yeast starter culture by combining the wine yeast, pectic enzyme, yeast nutrient, and orange juice. Cover, shake vigorously, and let stand 1 to 3 hours, until bubbly; then add to the must.

3. Add the acid blend. Pour the mixture into a 2-gallon (7.6 L) plastic bucket or wastebasket, cover loosely, and let sit for one week. Rack the liquid to a 1-gallon (3.8 L) airlocked fermentation vessel. Rack as needed to clear the wine. When fermentation has stopped, rack the wine into bottles, cork, and cellar.

4. Wait six months before sampling.

Tomato Wine

This wine will be golden to orange, even though the tomatoes are red. Most of the color is in the pulp, not the juice. You'll be wasting your time if you try to make this wine from those hard little baseballs that masquerade as tomatoes in the supermarket. Use the biggest, reddest, juiciest tomatoes you can find in the garden or the farm market. Taste them before you use them in your wine. Some of the giant varieties are low in acid, and that's fine. Their sweet, mellow flavor will be enhanced by the apple juice and citrus juice. Tannin is essential in this recipe for the proper "mouth feel."

YIELD: 1 GALLON (3.8 L)

3 pounds (1.4 kg) juicy red ripe tomatoes

12 ounces (360 ml) apple juice concentrate

2 pounds (900 g) white sugar

1 Campden tablet (optional)

1 package (5–7 g) Montrachet wine yeast

1 teaspoon (5 g) pectic enzyme

1 teaspoon (5 g) yeast nutrient

1½ cups (360 ml) orange juice, at room temperature

¼ teaspoon (1.25 g) tannin

1. Mash the tomatoes in a large stainless steel pot. Add 2 quarts (1.9 L) of water and bring to a boil. Add the apple juice concentrate and sugar, and boil for 5 more minutes. Transfer the mixture to a 2-gallon (7.6 L) plastic wastebasket or bucket, and add 1 quart (about 1 L) of water. Add a Campden tablet, if desired, and let the mixture sit, loosely covered, for 24 hours.

2. In a jar, make a yeast starter culture by combining the wine yeast, pectic enzyme, yeast nutrient, and orange juice. Cover, shake vigorously, and let stand 1 to 3 hours, until bubbly; then add to the must.

3. Add the tannin, and ferment for five days, punching down the cap daily to help provide oxygen. Then rack the liquid from the must into a 1-gallon (3.8 L) airlocked fermentation vessel, and let the mixture ferment for three to four months. Bottle, cork, and cellar the wine.

4. Wait six months before sampling.

Vegetable Medley Wine

You probably cook with fermented products — teriyaki sauce, soy sauce, and various wines, for example — and this wine serves the same purpose. It draws its flavors from that divine trio of vegetables — celery, onions, and carrots. Add some citrus, raisins, and a touch of cayenne, and you have a marinade and basting liquid that will turn almost any meat dish into a feast. We're willing to bet that you'll get repeated requests for this lively liquid — for cooking, not for sipping. You may find that it is a very popular gift for the gourmet cook in your circle of friends.

YIELD: 1 GALLON (3.8 L)

3 pounds (1.4 kg) carrots, sliced

2 pounds (900 g) celery, sliced

1 cup (240 ml) chopped onions

⅛ teaspoon (.625 g) cayenne pepper

Juice of 2 large oranges

1 teaspoon (5 g) orange zest

8 ounces (240 g) golden raisins, chopped

2½ pounds (1.14 kg) white sugar

1 Campden tablet (optional)

1 package (5–7 g) Montrachet wine yeast

1 teaspoon (5 g) pectic enzyme

1 teaspoon (5 g) yeast nutrient

1½ cups (360 ml) orange juice, at room temperature

1. Put the vegetables in a large stainless steel pot with the cayenne and enough water to cover. Simmer until the vegetables are tender. Strain the vegetables from the liquid, reserving 1 cup (240 ml) of vegetables for later use. Stir the juice of 2 oranges, the orange zest, raisins, and sugar into the liquid; then remove from the heat.

2. Crush the reserved vegetables into a paste, and stir them back into the liquid. Transfer the mixture to a 2-gallon (7.6 L) plastic bucket or wastebasket, add water until the volume is approximately 1 gallon (3.8 L), and let cool. Add a Campden tablet, if desired. Let the mixture sit, loosely covered, for 24 hours.

3. In a jar, make a yeast starter culture by combining the wine yeast, pectic enzyme, yeast nutrient, and the 1½ cups (360 ml) orange juice. Cover, shake vigorously, and let stand 1 to 3 hours, until bubbly; then add to the must. Rack into a 1-gallon (3.8 L) airlocked fermentation vessel and ferment for three to four months, racking to clear. Bottle, cork, and cellar the wine.

4. Wait six months before sampling.

Sweet Wheat Wine

This wine is light and lively with hints of citrus and a nice, vinous character. The wheat supplies nutrients and sugars to enhance the fermentation process.

YIELD: 1 GALLON (3.8 L)

- ¾ pound (340 g) wheat berries
- 1 pound (450 g) raisins *or* 1 pint (480 ml) white grape juice concentrate
- 2½ pounds (1.14 kg) brown sugar
- 1 Campden tablet (optional)
- 1 package (5–7 g) wine yeast
- 1 teaspoon (5 g) pectic enzyme
- 1 teaspoon (5 g) yeast nutrient
- 1½ cups (360 ml) orange juice, at room temperature
- 1 ounce (30 g) citric acid

1. Soak the wheat berries overnight in ½ quart (500 ml) of water to soften them. Mince the wheat berries and raisins (in a food processor) and transfer them to a 2-gallon (7.6 L) plastic container. Bring 2 quarts (1.9 L) of water to a boil, pour it over the wheat–raisin mixture, add the brown sugar, and let cool. Add a Campden tablet, if desired, and let sit, well covered, for 24 hours.

2. In a jar, make a yeast starter culture by combining the wine yeast, pectic enzyme, yeast nutrient, and orange juice. Cover, shake vigorously, and let stand 1 to 3 hours, until bubbly; then add to the must.

3. Add the citric acid; then let the mixture sit, loosely covered, for ten days, stirring daily. Rack the mixture to a 2-gallon (7.6 L) airlocked fermentation vessel and allow it to ferment to completion. When fermentation stops, bottle, cork, and cellar the wine.

4. Wait at least six months before sampling.

Chapter Four

MAKING MEADS, MELOMELS & METHEGLINS

D id you ever notice how many heroines of romantic fiction have "kisses sweeter than wine" and "lips that taste like honey"? In England during the Middle Ages, newly married couples were given a month's worth of mead to drink to ensure that the couple would bear fruit quickly, hence the term "honeymoon." Mead is widely acknowledged as the world's oldest alcoholic beverage. Its rich history transcends time and cultures.

Both honey and wine spark the imagination with images of things delicious and desirable. If you've never understood just why that is so, you probably haven't been lucky enough to sample meads, melomels, and metheglins, three kinds of honey wines that you can create in myriad combinations.

Honey wines are usually full-bodied and delicious — enjoyable with poultry as an entreé, with desserts, or as a creative addition to any of your favorite recipes that call for wine. And they are not difficult to make once you understand their special requirements.

Dry Mead. Dry meads have no flavoring other than honey and contain about 2½ pounds (1.14 kg) of honey per gallon (3.8 L) of mead.

Sack Mead. The most historic form of mead, sack mead is sweeter than other meads, but again, honey is the only flavoring agent. The honey content is usually about 4 pounds (1.8 kg) per gallon (3.8 L) of mead.

Small Mead. This variety is for the impatient. It contains less honey and ferments more quickly than other meads. A small mead contains from 1 to 1½ pounds (450 to 675 g) of honey per gallon (3.8 L) of mead. Ale yeast usually starts the fermentation of a small mead, which is generally completed within one week. Small meads are more like ale than like wine.

Metheglin. Similar to sack meads, metheglins develop more complex flavors through the addition of herbs and spices. The recipes for these mixtures of herbs and spices, called gruits, were jealously guarded by monks of the Middle Ages.

Mulsum or Melomel. Meads made with fruit for additional flavoring are called mulsums or melomels. A few varieties appear below, but the numbers of melomels are limited only by your imagination.

- *Cyser.* A sack mead made with honey and apples, this mead variation is closely related to hard cider.

- *Morat.* A sack mead made with mulberries.

- *Pyment.* A mead made with a mixture of honey and grape juice.

- *Hippocras.* A pyment with spices added.

- *Rhodamel.* A mead made with rose petals.

- *Fortified Meads.* Meads that are enhanced with brandy or vodka, giving them a higher alcohol content.

SOME KEY INGREDIENTS

A successful mead depends on three key ingredients: honey, water, and acid. Some meads also need tannins to keep them from being too insipidly sweet.

Honey

Fresh honey, with the least processing possible, is best for making meads. If possible, buy raw unprocessed honey from a local beekeeper and use it quickly; the quality of honey deteriorates over time. Experiment with different kinds of honey, because the results will vary. Orange-blossom honey is good for making traditional meads; clover honey is good for flavored meads.

Different kinds of honey have slightly different flavors, but unless there are stores that specialize in different varieties nearby, you may find that only certain honeys are available where you live. Don't despair. If you have a choice, taste the honey and pick your favorite. If only commercial honey is available, it may be a blend of several varieties. Use it anyway; the results will still be delicious.

Because honey is low in nitrogen, and nitrogen is required for a vigorous fermentation, we recommend that you add a yeast nutrient to all meads, including melomels, even though they get some nitrogen from their fruit components. Experts disagree about the treatment of honey when making meads. The traditional method is to boil the honey with water at the beginning of the process to coagulate the proteins and the beeswax residue that is often present. The foamy residue is then skimmed from the surface. (In addition, boiling kills any wild yeast that may be present.) The process usually results in clear mead without any additional treatment of the wine. Some critics point out, however, that boiling the honey with water removes some of the honey's aroma, and thus decreases the quality of the mead. They suggest bringing the honey-water mixture to a temperature of 150°F (66°C), holding this temperature for 5 minutes, and then rapidly cooling the mixture to room temperature, which will preserve most of the volatile aromatic components. Others choose to avoid heat completely, using sulfites to sterilize the must and worrying about clarifying the mead only prior to bottling. All of these methods, in our experience, result in delicious meads. Experiment to determine which method you prefer.

Water

The kind of water you use is also important. Some old recipes call for rainwater, which once was virtually pure. Today, rainwater often contains pollutants, such as those in acid rain. Some springwater, also a favorite in mead recipes, has a high sodium content, as does softened water. Your safest bet is probably to use boiled tap water, but if your water supply is high in iron, calcium, or other minerals, you may opt for distilled water.

Acid Component

Meads need an added acid component. Most winemakers use either a commercial acid blend or some citrus juice to give the wine its necessary tartness. The acid source can be added at the beginning of the fermentation or at the end. If you are a novice, closely follow the recipes in this chapter until you get comfortable with making meads. As you gain experience, you may wish to adjust the acidity of your meads at the end of the process. The acid level of a finished mead should be between 0.5 and 0.7 percent, depending on your taste.

RECIPE CATEGORIES

As you look at the recipes for these honey wines, you'll think that the distinctions among the kinds of meads seem pretty academic. For convenience, we treat the different kinds of honey wines as though the categories were separate and distinct. But we bet it never occurred to early winemakers to worry about such distinctions. Like Dom Perignon, who blended wines to achieve the flavors he wanted, early mead makers were interested in good-tasting wines. Dom Perignon became the romantic figure of champagne fame because he experimented until he found the perfect combinations of flavors to suit his taste. In the process, he showed champagne makers how to achieve consistently fine wines.

Making Meads

Made correctly, mead has good body and great flavor. If you decide to buy winemaking ingredients from a commercial source, you'll need three major ingredients in addition to honey and water — yeast, yeast nutrient, and acid blend. The yeast nutrient contains ammonium compounds, trace elements, and vitamins. Citric acid (or acid blend) gives the wine the acid component that's necessary for good wine flavor and helps create a good environment for yeast

NOTE

Mead recipes begin on page 105

growth. It also has a slight preservative action. Because commercial yeast nutrients vary somewhat according to the source, use the amount of yeast nutrient recommended by the supplier. You can vary the amount of acid you add according to your taste once you have some experience. Whatever amount you use, though, be sure to write down the blend so you can duplicate it, just in case you've achieved the perfect mead. Record the amount of fruit additives, too. Your wine will still be a mead as long as the taste of honey is preserved.

Basic Mead Techniques. The simplest way to make a natural mead is to add a 6-ounce (180 ml) can of citrus fruit juice concentrate for every 1 gallon (3.8 L) of honey wine. The concentrate provides both nutrients and acidity, but it also affects the taste. Since most commercial citrus juices are made from the whole fruit, which contains some of the bitter components located just beneath the peels, you could pick up some unwanted bitterness using this method. A better method is to fresh-squeeze the juice and add the finely grated outer rind for flavor, being careful not to include any of the bitter inner rind.

Nutrients to feed the wine yeast can also come from grain (such as wheat), other fruits (grapes, for example), or vegetables (like potatoes). Any of these let the yeast grow properly. When you pick a natural yeast nutrient, be sure you consider how much acid is present in it. If your nutrient source is low in acid, the juice of a couple of lemons or oranges or some acid blend will work well to give your wine tartness. Finally, pectic enzyme digests the pectin in fruits and the waxy substances in honey, which are notorious for causing cloudy wines. Using it will ensure that you don't end up with a tasty but unattractive mead.

Making Melomels

Some of the best wines we've ever tried are melomels. The combination of honey and fruit flavors produces a fruity, tangy wine with a lovely bouquet and a sound body. The different flavors of melomels are limited only by the fruits you have available. They're perfect for home gardeners who have a choice of fruits harvested from their own backyard berry patch or orchard. The marriage of fruit and honey solves the yeast-nutrient problem that occurs when making wines with honey only. If the fruit used to make wine is low in acid, the juice of three citrus fruits — one lemon and two oranges, for example — provides the necessary acid. If you are just starting out, we strongly suggest that you try at least one melomel. Once you have, a whole new world of fine wines becomes available to you — and they're easy to make, so you're almost certain to succeed.

Basic Melomel Techniques. The general method we use to develop recipes yielding 1 gallon (3.8 L) of melomel is to start with 3 pounds (1.4 kg) of honey, 1 to 3 pounds (.45 to 1.4 kg) of fresh fruit, and citrus juice, if required. Melomels may be as difficult to clear as meads, so we generally boil the honey in two times its volume of water for approximately 10 to 20 minutes and skim off the foam that rises to the surface. Eliminating these waxy impurities helps keep the wine clear. Adding pectic enzyme helps too. Cloudy wine is not harmful to drink, but the clear, sparkling color of properly cleared wine, served in crystal-clear glasses, is part of a wine's charm.

After you've finished this first step, add the fruit to the still-hot mixture, let cool, and add a Campden tablet, if desired. Allow the mixture to set for 24 hours, both for the action of the Campden tablet to stop and to allow the full fruit flavor to permeate the mixture. Then add a yeast starter culture and some tannin, if called for. Allow the wine to ferment, covered, for about 10 days. After the first vigorous fermentation, transfer the wine to an airlocked container so the fermentation can continue, racking as needed to clear the wine.

Allowing some of the smaller fruit fragments to enter the airlocked container provides nutrients for yeast growth. Rack the wine after three months, and continue to rack as needed to clear the wine. You'll need to wait at least six months before bottling it and another six months before sampling, but these times are approximate. If bubbles are present after moving the wine to a warm room for 24 hours, your wine isn't ready for bottling. Try again in a month. If the fermentation still isn't complete, wait another month. If a longer waiting period is necessary, be sure to rack the wine at least every three months until you bottle it. With each racking, the wine becomes clearer and more beautiful. Your friends will love these wines, so be

NOTE

Melomel recipes begin on page 109

sure to make an extra batch for creative gift-giving.

In this chapter you'll find some of our favorite melomel recipes, but don't be limited by them. Experiment. Creating rich-flavored melomels to your own taste is part of the fun of winemaking. When we looked for old country wine recipes, collecting family favorites from amateur winemakers and creating some of our own, we made dozens of melomels. Our "panel of experts" — friends and family members who were more than willing to attend an occasional wine tasting — chose these recipes as their favorites.

Making Metheglins

Metheglins, the honey-based wines flavored with herbs or spices, are as varied as the people who make them. Some fine wines with excellent bouquets result from fermenting honey with herbs or spices. But there is no complete list of metheglins. They may be simple, consisting of a single herb combined with honey, water, yeast, and appropriate nutrients, or they may be complex, with a multitude of ingredients.

Of all the wines we researched and developed, we think metheglins are the most exciting. If you've already discovered the pleasure of growing herbs, the step to using herbs in winemaking is a natural extension of your cooking experiments with Mother Nature's seasonings.

COOKING WITH METHEGLINS

The wines made from honey and herbs or spices stimulate the palate as drinks, but they really come into their own as cooking wines — imparting their subtle charm to recipes that many of us may have tasted and tried in vain to duplicate. If you've tried a honey glaze for ham or fowl — or even whole roasted salmon — and found the honey flavor too strong, metheglins might change your mind about honey in cooking. The honey and herbs in metheglins are always subtle, never overpowering. The wines seems to penetrate the meat, fowl, and fish with subtle flavors that may earn you a reputation as "the best cook in town." Our friends still talk about our annual Christmas party turkey, which we baste and inject with both sage metheglin and natural mead.

To acquaint you with some of the possibilities that exist for making metheglins, we prepared a list of herbs and spices used in these wines. The list is by no means exhaustive — we urge you to experiment. Just be sure to check the properties of the herb before you make a metheglin from it. Hayfever sufferers, for example, might be well advised to stay away from chamomile metheglin, which contains an herb from the same botanical family as ragweed — a less flavorful branch on the family tree. Chamomile tea has long been recommended as a relaxing bedtime beverage, but when I adopted it as my favorite nightcap, I became the most relaxed, but stuffy-nosed, member of my family. Knowing that, I haven't even been tempted to sample chamomile metheglin, even though its slightly perfumey bouquet tempts less allergic members of my family.

Basic Metheglin Techniques. How much of any flavoring component you will use in a metheglin depends on the nature of the wine and the use you intend for it. Start by making a fairly strong tea from the herb, and then make the tea into a honey-based wine. For cooking wines, you may need a slightly stronger tea. Metheglins are short on effort and long on flavor. And there is a great variety in the kinds of herbs and spices used for them. Depending on growing conditions, fresh herbs vary widely in the strength of the flavorful essential oils that account for their taste. Treat herbs well, giving them the proper soil and plenty of water, and they are likely to be milder and less flavorful

METHEGLIN FLAVORINGS

Almonds	Fennel root	Orange blossoms	Sweet basil
Angelica	Ginger	Orange mint	Sweet marjoram
Balm	Honeysuckle	Orange peel	Sweet woodruff
Caraway seeds	Hyssop	Parsley	Tarragon (French)
Cardamom	Juniper berries	Peppermint	Thyme
Chamomile	Lemon balm	Rosemary	Vanilla
Cinnamon stick	Lemon mint	Rose petals	Violet
Clover blossom	Lemon peel	Sage	
Cloves (whole)	Mace	Spearmint	
Dandelions	Nutmeg		

than herbs grown in poor, dry soil. Remember that flavors in dried herbs are more concentrated. The list of metheglin flavorings (see page 102) will help you gauge just a few of the possibilities.

Because neither the honey nor the herbs and spices in metheglins provide the necessary nutrients for full fermentation, older metheglin recipes usually include a couple of oranges and a lemon or some other citrus fruit. We usually add yeast nutrients to metheglins when we don't want to add citrus. In other varieties, the citrus seems to enhance the flavor of the herb or spice. When you are ready to develop your own recipes, think about the flavors you like and vary your ingredients accordingly. Just remember, if you use yeast nutrient, you also need to add acid blend.

To help you to develop your own special metheglins, consult the chart on page 104 to help you with the correct proportions of the flavoring ingredients. Because the amounts of flavoring components used in making metheglins vary according to taste, you might decide the flavor is too strong. In that case, simply blend the metheglin with other vintages of meads or melomels until you have adjusted the metheglin to the subtle flavor characteristics that suit you. You can also mix metheglins with fruit wines and fruit juices to make exciting wine coolers.

Herbal wines and meads have been made for centuries by monks. The secret and solitary nature of their activities gives metheglins their historic mystique. Maybe the next Chartreuse has already been created in the kitchen of some amateur winemaker who experimented with herbs found in a backyard herb garden. If you aren't quite ready for that distinction, start by trying some of our metheglin recipes.

NOTE

Metheglin recipes begin on page 122

Proportion of Metheglin Ingredients

Ingredient	Proportion
FLAVORINGS	
Cinnamon sticks	½ ounce (15 g) per gallon (3.8 L)
Dried herbs	2 to 3 ounces (60–90 g) per gallon (3.8 L), loosely packed
Fresh herbs	2 to 3 cups (480–600 ml) per gallon (3.8 L), loosely packed
Juniper berries	4 to 5 per gallon (3.8 L) *Note: Juniper berries are one of the flavoring components of gin — and a few go a very long way!*
Nuts	1 to 2 ounces (30–60 g) per gallon (3.8 L)
Peels (citrus)	2 to 3 fruits per gallon (3.8 L) *Note: Just the absolute outer rind.*
NUTRIENTS	
Acid blend	1 to 3 teaspoons (5–15 g) per gallon (3.8 L)
Citrus fruits	3 per gallon (3.8 L)
Grape concentrate	1 cup (240 ml) per gallon (3.8 L)
Grapes, fresh	2 pounds (900 g) per gallon (3.8 L)
Grape juice	32 ounces (1 L) per gallon (3.8 L)
Other fruits	Varies
Raisins	1 pound (450 g) per gallon (3.8 L)
Yeast nutrient	1 teaspoon (5 g) per gallon (3.8 L)

Dry Mead

This is a good recipe for beginning mead makers. It gives fine results from a relatively simple process. But beware: You may succumb to its allure and become an avid mead maker.

YIELD: 1 GALLON (3.8 L)

2½ pounds (1.14 kg) orange-blossom honey

1 teaspoon (5 g) acid blend

1 teaspoon (5 g) pectic enzyme

1 Campden tablet (optional)

1 package (5–7 g) Montrachet yeast

1 teaspoon (5 g) yeast nutrient

1½ cups (360 ml) orange juice, at room temperature

¼ teaspoon (1.25 g) grape tannin

1. In a large enamel or stainless steel pot, boil the honey in water (1 part honey to 2 parts water — use the empty honey jar to measure the water) for 10 to 20 minutes, skimming off any foam that forms. (The foam will contain water impurities and beeswax residue.)

2. Let cool, and then transfer the honey mixture to a 2-gallon (7.6 L) plastic container. Add the acid, pectic enzyme, and enough water to make 1 gallon (3.8 L). Add the Campden tablet, if desired, and let the mixture sit, well covered, for 24 hours.

3. In a jar, make a yeast starter culture by combining the yeast, yeast nutrient, and orange juice. Cover, shake vigorously, and let stand 1 to 3 hours, until bubbly; then add to the must.

4. Add the tannin and allow the mixture to ferment for five to ten days. We recommend racking meads after the most vigorous fermentation; siphon the wine into a 1-gallon (3.8 L) airlocked fermentation vessel. In three months, rack into another airlocked container. After about six months, rack into another airlocked container. Rack again right before bottling — about a year after fermentation started. Then bottle and cork the finished mead, and store it in a cool cellar.

5. Age for at least six months before opening a bottle.

Sack Mead

If you like your meads sweet, light, and true to their heritage, you'll love sack mead. The flavor is so full of honey, you can almost hear the bees buzz! Because this mead is flavored only with honey, the tannin is an essential part of the recipe. Leave it out, and you may find the end result a bit insipid. Budding wine connoisseurs often choose sack mead for a little Renaissance flair.

YIELD: 1 GALLON (3.8 L)

3 pounds (1.4 kg) orange-blossom honey

1 teaspoon (5 g) acid blend

1 teaspoon (5 g) pectic enzyme

1 Campden tablet (optional)

1 package (5–7 g) Montrachet yeast

1 teaspoon (5 g) yeast nutrient

1½ cups (360 ml) orange juice, at room temperature

¼ teaspoon (1.25 g) grape tannin

1. In a large enamel or stainless steel pot, boil the honey in water (1 part honey to 2 parts water) for 10 to 20 minutes, skimming off any foam that forms. (The foam will contain water impurities and beeswax residue.)

2. Let cool, and then transfer the honey mixture to a 2-gallon (7.6 L) plastic container. Add the acid, pectic enzyme, and enough water to make 1 gallon (3.8 L). Add the Campden tablet, if desired, and let the mixture sit, well covered, for 24 hours.

3. In a jar, make a yeast starter culture by combining the yeast, yeast nutrient, and orange juice. Cover, shake vigorously, and let stand 1 to 3 hours, until bubbly; then add to the must.

4. Add the tannin and allow the mixture to ferment. We recommend racking meads after the most vigorous fermentation; siphon the wine into a 1-gallon (3.8 L) airlocked fermentation vessel. In about three months, rack into another airlocked container. In about six months, rack once again. Rack a final time right before bottling — about a year after fermentation started. Then bottle and cork the finished mead, and store it in a cool cellar.

5. Age for at least six months before opening a bottle.

Natural Sack Mead

The raisins in this recipe give the mead a vinous quality that is more pronounced than in the previous sack mead recipe. Why not try both?

YIELD: 1 GALLON (3.8 L)

3½ pounds (1.6 kg) clover honey

2 ounces (60 g) golden raisins

1 teaspoon (5 g) acid blend

1 teaspoon (5 g) pectic enzyme

1 cup (240 ml) jasmine tea

1 Campden tablet (optional)

1 package (5–7 g) sweet mead yeast

1 teaspoon (5 g) yeast nutrient

1½ cups (360 ml) orange juice, at room temperature

¼ teaspoon (1.25 g) grape tannin

1. In a large enamel or stainless steel pot, boil the honey in water (1 part honey to 2 parts water) for 10 to 20 minutes, skimming off any foam that forms. Mince the raisins and add to the must.

2. Let the mixture cool, and then transfer it to a 2-gallon (7.6 L) plastic container. Add the acid, pectic enzyme, jasmine tea, and enough water to make 1 gallon (3.8 L). Add the Campden tablet, if desired, and let the mixture sit, well covered, for 24 hours.

3. In a jar, make a yeast starter culture by combining the yeast, yeast nutrient, and orange juice. Cover, shake vigorously, and let stand 1 to 3 hours, until bubbly; then add to the must.

4. Add the tannin and allow the mixture to ferment. We recommend racking meads after the most vigorous fermentation; siphon the wine into a 1-gallon (3.8 L) airlocked fermentation vessel. In about three months, rack into another airlocked container. In about six months, rack once again. Rack a final time right before bottling — about a year after fermentation started. Then bottle and cork the finished mead, and store it in a cool cellar.

5. Age for at least six months before opening a bottle.

Sweet Dessert Mead

This is a golden nectar to serve with your most luscious dessert — a fitting finish to any elegant meal. **Optional:** *You may fortify this wine by adding 1 to 2 cups (240 to 280 ml) of brandy to improve aging and keeping qualities.*

YIELD: 1 GALLON (3.8 L)

4 pounds (1.8 kg) tupelo honey

1 teaspoon (5 g) orange zest

1 cup (240 ml) jasmine tea

1 teaspoon (5 g) acid blend

1 teaspoon (5 g) pectic enzyme

1 Campden tablet (optional)

1 package (5–7 g) Montrachet yeast

1 teaspoon (5 g) yeast nutrient

1½ cups (360 ml) orange juice, at room temperature

⅛ teaspoon (.625 g) grape tannin

1. In a large enamel or stainless steel pot, boil the honey in water (1 part honey to 2 parts water — use the empty honey jar to measure the water) for 10 to 20 minutes, skimming off any foam that forms.

2. Let the mixture cool, and then transfer it to a 2-gallon (7.6 L) plastic container. Add the orange zest, tea, acid, pectic enzyme, and enough water to make 1 gallon (3.8 L). Add the Campden tablet, if desired, and let the mixture sit, well covered, for 24 hours.

3. In a jar, make a yeast starter culture by combining the yeast, yeast nutrient, and orange juice. Cover, shake vigorously, and let stand 1 to 3 hours, until bubbly; then add to the must.

4. Add the tannin and allow the mixture to ferment. We recommend racking meads after the most vigorous fermentation; siphon the wine into a 1-gallon (3.8 L) airlocked fermentation vessel. In about three months, rack into another airlocked container. In about six months, rack once again. Rack a final time right before bottling — about a year after fermentation started. Then bottle and cork the finished mead, and store it in a cool cellar.

5. Age for at least six months before opening a bottle.

Apple Melomel

This is an old, old wine, popular in Europe long before pioneer families brewed it and long before it was given the name "Applejack" and became the stuff of country and western music.

YIELD: 1 GALLON (3.8 L)

3 pounds (1.4 kg) honey

1 gallon (3.8 L) apple cider (use fresh cider, without preservatives, which would inhibit the fermentation process)

1 teaspoon (5 g) acid blend

1 teaspoon (5 g) pectic enzyme

1 package (5–7 g) champagne yeast

1 teaspoon (5 g) yeast nutrient

1½ cups (360 ml) orange juice, at room temperature

1. In a large enamel or stainless steel pot, boil the honey in water (1 part honey to 2 parts water — use the empty honey jar to measure the water) for 10 to 20 minutes, skimming off any foam that forms. Let the mixture cool, and then transfer it to a 2-gallon (7.6 L) plastic container. Add the cider, acid, and pectic enzyme. Add the Campden tablet, if desired, and let the mixture sit, well covered, for 24 hours.

2. In a jar, make a yeast starter culture by combining the yeast, yeast nutrient, and orange juice. Cover, shake vigorously, and let stand 1 to 3 hours, until bubbly; then add to the must.

3. Allow the mixture to ferment. We recommend racking after the most vigorous fermentation; siphon the wine into a 1-gallon (3.8 L) airlocked fermentation vessel, topping off with additional apple cider if necessary. In about three months, rack into another airlocked container. In about six months, rack once again. Rack a final time right before bottling — about a year after fermentation started. Then bottle and cork the finished melomel, and store it in a cool cellar.

4. Age for at least six months before opening a bottle.

VARIATION: Spiced Apple Melomel

Add a cinnamon stick to the liquid in step 1, and remove it later from the cooked mixture.

Blackberry Melomel

Blackberry melomel is a bit denser and darker in color than other fruit melomels.

YIELD: 1 GALLON (3.8 L)

3 pounds (1.4 kg) blackberries

1 cup (225 g) sugar

Juice of 1 lemon

1 teaspoon (5 g) lemon zest

3 bags blackberry tea

2 pounds (900 g) raspberry honey

⅛ teaspoon (.625 g) grape tannin

1 teaspoon (5 g) acid blend

1 teaspoon (5 g) pectic enzyme

1 Campden tablet (optional)

1 package (5–7 g) Montrachet yeast

1 teaspoon (5 g) yeast nutrient

1½ cups (360 ml) orange juice, at room temperature

1. Crush the blackberries and transfer them to a 2-gallon (7.6 L) plastic container. Add the sugar, lemon juice, and lemon zest. Put the tea bags in 1 cup (240 ml) of boiling water and steep for 5 minutes. In a large enamel or stainless steel pot, boil the honey in water (1 part honey to 2 parts water) for 10 to 20 minutes, skimming off any foam that forms.

2. Pour the honey mixture over the berries and add the brewed tea and grape tannin. Let the mixture cool. Add the acid, pectic enzyme, and enough water to make 1 gallon (3.8 L). Add the Campden tablet, if desired, and let the mixture sit, well covered, for 24 hours.

3. In a jar, make a yeast starter culture by combining the yeast, yeast nutrient, and orange juice. Cover, shake vigorously, and let stand 1 to 3 hours, until bubbly; then add to the must.

4. Allow the mixture to ferment. We recommend racking melomels after the most vigorous fermentation; siphon the wine into a 1-gallon (3.8 L) airlocked fermentation vessel. In about three months, rack into another airlocked container. In about six months, rack once again. Rack a final time right before bottling — about a year after fermentation started. Bottle and cork the finished melomel, and store it in a cool cellar.

5. Age for at least six months before opening a bottle.

Blueberry Melomel

You'll love the fresh flavor of this melomel, along with its deep color. Serve it in crystal-clear wineglasses for best effect.

YIELD: 1 GALLON (3.8 L)

1 quart (1 L) fresh blueberries

1 cup (225 g) white sugar

Juice of 1 lemon

1 teaspoon (5 g) lemon zest

2 pounds (900 g) wildflower honey

1 teaspoon (5 g) acid blend

1 teaspoon (5 g) pectic enzyme

1 Campden tablet (optional)

1 package (5–7 g) Montrachet yeast

1 teaspoon (5 g) yeast nutrient

1½ cups (360 ml) orange juice, at room temperature

¼ teaspoon (1.25 g) grape tannin

1. Crush the berries in a 2-gallon (7.6 L) plastic container. Add the sugar, lemon juice, and lemon zest. In a large enamel or stainless steel pot, boil the honey in water (1 part honey to 2 parts water — use the empty honey jar to measure the water) for 10 to 20 minutes, skimming off any foam that forms. (The foam will contain water impurities and beeswax residue.)

2. Pour the honey mixture over the fruit. Add the acid, the pectic enzyme, and enough water to make 1 gallon (3.8 L). Add the Campden tablet, if desired, and let the mixture sit, well covered, for 24 hours.

3. In a jar, make a yeast starter culture by combining the yeast, yeast nutrient, and orange juice. Cover, shake vigorously, and let stand 1 to 3 hours, until bubbly; then add to the must.

4. Add the tannin and allow the mixture to ferment. We recommend racking after the most vigorous fermentation; siphon the wine into a 1-gallon (3.8 L) airlocked fermentation vessel. In about three months, rack into another airlocked container. In about six months, rack once again. Rack a final time right before bottling — about a year after fermentation started. Then bottle and cork the finished melomel, and store it in a cool cellar.

5. Age for at least six months before opening a bottle.

Cherry Melomel

During Rich's first forays into winemaking, he made a number of different kinds of wines. The cherry melomel, however, was among the first wines he opened when the long waiting period was over, and he was hooked. Cherry melomel has every-thing: attractive, clear red color; flavor that is a complex blend of cherries and honey; a pleasant bouquet; and a lovely, lingering aftertaste that seduces with every sip. You won't find it in your local wine store, however; you have to make it yourself. You may want to make several batches — it won't last long.

YIELD: 1 GALLON (3.8 L)

3 pounds (1.4 kg) clover honey

1 pound (450 g) dark or sour cherries, halved, with pits

1 teaspoon (5 g) acid blend

1 teaspoon (5 g) pectic enzyme

1 Campden tablet (optional)

1 package (5–7 g) champagne yeast

1 teaspoon (5 g) yeast nutrient

1½ cups (360 ml) orange juice, at room temperature

1. In a large enamel or stainless steel pot, boil the honey in water (1 part honey to 2 parts water — use the empty honey jar to measure the water) for 10 to 20 minutes, skimming off any foam that forms. (The foam will contain water impurities and beeswax residue.) Put the cherries in a 2-gallon (7.6 L) plastic container. Pour the honey mixture over the fruit and let cool.

2. Add the acid, pectic enzyme, and enough water to make 1 gallon (3.8 L). Add the Campden tablet, if desired, and let the mixture sit, well covered, for 24 hours.

3. In a jar, make a yeast starter culture by combining the yeast, yeast nutrient, and orange juice. Cover, shake vigorously, and let stand 1 to 3 hours, until bubbly; then add to the must.

4. Allow the mixture to ferment. We recommend racking after the most vigor-ous fermentation; siphon the wine into a 1-gallon (3.8 L) airlocked fermen-tation vessel. In about three months, rack into another airlocked container. In about six months, rack once again. Rack a final time right before bottling — about a year after fermentation started. Then bottle and cork the finished melomel, and store it in a cool cellar.

5. Age for at least six months before opening a bottle.

Cranberry Melomel

Cranberries never tasted better or looked prettier than in this sparkling melomel. We like to serve this mead to our favorite valentines with little wedges of Gouda cheese and juicy green grapes.

YIELD: 1 GALLON (3.8 L)

1½ pounds (675 g) fresh cranberries

1 cup (225 g) white sugar

Juice of 1 large orange

1 tablespoon (15 g) freshly grated orange zest

2 pounds (900 g) orange-blossom honey

1 teaspoon (5 g) pectic enzyme

1 Campden tablet (optional)

1 package (5–7 g) Montrachet yeast

1 teaspoon (5 g) yeast nutrient

1½ cups (360 ml) orange juice, at room temperature

¼ teaspoon (1.25 g) grape tannin

1. Wash the berries and mash thoroughly. Put the crushed berries in a 2-gallon (7.6 L) plastic container, and sprinkle the sugar over them. Add the juice from the orange and the orange zest. In a large enamel or stainless steel pot, boil the honey in water (1 part honey to 2 parts water — use the empty honey jar to measure the water) for 10 to 20 minutes, skimming off any foam that forms. Pour the honey mixture over the fruit and let cool.

2. Add the pectic enzyme and enough water to make 1 gallon (3.8 L). Add the Campden tablet, if desired, and let the mixture sit, well covered, for 24 hours.

3. In a jar, make a yeast starter culture by combining the yeast, yeast nutrient, and the 1½ cups (360 ml) orange juice. Cover, shake vigorously, and let stand 1 to 3 hours, until bubbly; then add to the must.

4. Add the tannin and allow the mixture to ferment. We recommend racking after the most vigorous fermentation; siphon the wine into a 1-gallon (3.8 L) airlocked fermentation vessel. In about three months, rack into another airlocked container. In about six months, rack once again. Rack a final time right before bottling — about a year after fermentation started. Then bottle and cork the finished melomel, and store it in a cool cellar.

5. Age for at least six months before opening a bottle.

Grape Melomel (Pyment)

This purple wine, historically known as pyment, was popular in ancient Egypt. The honey mellows the Concord flavor, but the wine keeps its deep color if you leave the skins on the grape; for a lighter wine, remove and discard the grape skins before using the grapes.

YIELD: 1 GALLON (3.8 L)

3 pounds (1.4 kg) Concord grapes

3 pounds (1.4 kg) light honey

1 teaspoon (5 g) acid blend

1 teaspoon (5 g) pectic enzyme

1 Campden tablet (optional)

1 package (5–7 g) champagne yeast

1 teaspoon (5 g) yeast nutrient

1½ cups (360 ml) orange juice, at room temperature

1. Crush the grapes in a 2-gallon (7.6 L) plastic container. In a large enamel or stainless steel pot, boil the honey in water (1 part honey to 2 parts water — use the empty honey jar to measure the water) for 10 to 20 minutes, skimming off any foam that forms. (The foam will contain water impurities and beeswax residue.)

2. Pour the honey mixture over the grapes and let cool. Add the acid, pectic enzyme, and enough water to make 1 gallon (3.8 L). Add the Campden tablet, if desired, and let the mixture sit, well covered, for 24 hours.

3. In a jar, make a yeast starter culture by combining the yeast, yeast nutrient, and orange juice. Cover, shake vigorously, and let stand 1 to 3 hours, until bubbly; then add to the must.

4. Allow the mixture to ferment. We recommend racking after the most vigorous fermentation; siphon the wine into a 1-gallon (3.8 L) airlocked fermentation vessel. In about three months, rack into another airlocked container. In about six months, rack once again. Rack a final time right before bottling — about a year after fermentation started. Then bottle and cork the finished melomel, and store it in a cool cellar.

5. Age for at least six months before opening a bottle.

Kiwi Melomel

Kiwifruits have a flavor reminiscent of strawberries, but they're bigger, and they're relatively inexpensive. Just remove their fuzzy little skins, and you'll be surprised at how juicy they are. Don't worry about the tiny little seeds; they'll go right into the must. And you needn't worry about flavor: This wine is simply scrumptious.

YIELD: 1 GALLON (3.8 L)

3 pounds (1.4 kg) kiwifruit, peeled and coarsely chopped

1 cup (225 g) sugar

2½ pounds (1.14 kg) commercial honey

1 teaspoon (5 g) acid blend

1 teaspoon (5 g) pectic enzyme

1 Campden tablet (optional)

1 package (5–7 g) Montrachet yeast

1 teaspoon (5 g) yeast nutrient

1½ cups (360 ml) orange juice, at room temperature

¼ teaspoon (1.25 g) grape tannin

1. Put the kiwi and sugar into a 2-gallon (7.6 L) plastic container. In a large enamel or stainless steel pot, boil the honey in water (1 part honey to 2 parts water — use the empty honey jar to measure the water) for 10 to 20 minutes, skimming off any foam that forms. (The foam will contain water impurities and beeswax residue.)

2. Pour the honey mixture over the fruit and let cool. Add the acid, pectic enzyme, and enough water to make 1 gallon (3.8 L). Add the Campden tablet, if desired, and let the mixture sit, well covered, for 24 hours.

3. In a jar, make a yeast starter culture by combining the yeast, yeast nutrient, and orange juice. Cover, shake vigorously, and let stand 1 to 3 hours, until bubbly; then add to the must.

4. Add the tannin and allow the mixture to ferment. We recommend racking after the most vigorous fermentation; siphon the wine into a 1-gallon (3.8 L) airlocked fermentation vessel. In about three months, rack into another air-locked container. In about six months, rack once again. Rack a final time right before bottling — about a year after fermentation started. Then bottle and cork the finished melomel, and store it in a cool cellar.

5. Age for at least six months before opening a bottle.

Mulberry Melomel
(Morat)

Mulberries are not a popular table fruit — although kids love to eat them off the tree — because they are hard to pick and process. When you make a mulberry melomel, you don't have to worry about removing the tiny stems.

YIELD: 1 GALLON (3.8 L)

3 pounds (1.4 kg) mulberries

Juice of 1 large orange

Juice of 1 lemon

2 teaspoons (10 g) lemon zest

2½ pounds (1.14 kg) honey

1 teaspoon (5 g) acid blend

1 teaspoon (5 g) pectic enzyme

1 Campden tablet (optional)

1 package (5–7 g) Montrachet yeast

1 teaspoon (5 g) yeast nutrient

1½ cups (360 ml) orange juice, at room temperature

¼ teaspoon (1.25 g) grape tannin

1. Bruise the mulberries in a 2-gallon (7.6 L) plastic container. Add the juice of the orange and lemon and the lemon zest. In a large enamel or stainless steel pot, boil the honey in water (1 part honey to 2 parts water) for 10 to 20 minutes, skimming off any foam that forms.

2. Pour the honey mixture over the fruit and let cool. Add the acid, pectic enzyme, and enough water to make 1 gallon (3.8 L). Add the Campden tablet, if desired, and let the mixture sit, well covered, for 24 hours.

3. In a jar, make a yeast starter culture by combining the yeast, yeast nutrient, and the 1½ cups (360 ml) orange juice. Cover, shake vigorously, and let stand 1 to 3 hours, until bubbly; then add to the must.

4. Add the tannin and allow the mixture to ferment. We recommend racking after the most vigorous fermentation; siphon the wine into a 1-gallon (3.8 L) airlocked fermentation vessel. In about three months, rack into another airlocked container. In about six months, rack once again. Rack a final time right before bottling — about a year after fermentation started. Then bottle and cork the finished melomel, and store it in a cool cellar.

5. Age for at least six months before opening a bottle.

Peach Melomel

This melomel is golden and so fragrant that just opening the bottle will whet your appetite. It's lovely to sip, great in marinades and glazes for roast pork and chicken, and a perfect addition to iced teas and spritzers.

YIELD: 1 GALLON (3.8 L)

4 pounds (1.8 kg) peaches, washed, halved, and pitted

1 cup (225 g) sugar

Juice of 2 lemons

2 pounds (900 g) clover honey

1 teaspoon (5 g) acid blend

1 teaspoon (5 g) pectic enzyme

1 Campden tablet (optional)

1 package (5–7 g) Montrachet yeast

1 teaspoon (5 g) yeast nutrient

1½ cups (360 ml) orange juice, at room temperature

¼ teaspoon (1.25 g) grape tannin

1. Put the peaches, sugar, and lemon juice into a 2-gallon (7.6 L) plastic container. In a large enamel or stainless steel pot, boil the honey in water (1 part honey to 2 parts water — use the empty honey jar to measure the water) for 10 to 20 minutes, skimming off any foam that forms. (The foam will contain water impurities and beeswax residue.)

2. Pour the honey mixture over the fruit and let cool. Add the acid, pectic enzyme, and enough water to make 1 gallon (3.8 L). Add the Campden tablet, if desired, and let the mixture sit, well covered, for 24 hours.

3. In a jar, make a yeast starter culture by combining the yeast, yeast nutrient, and orange juice. Cover, shake vigorously, and let stand 1 to 3 hours, until bubbly; then add to the must.

4. Add the tannin and allow the mixture to ferment. We recommend racking after the most vigorous fermentation; siphon the wine into a 1-gallon (3.8 L) airlocked fermentation vessel. In about three months, rack into another airlocked container. In about six months, rack once again. Rack a final time right before bottling — about a year after fermentation started. Then bottle and cork the finished melomel, and store it in a cool cellar.

5. Age for at least six months before opening a bottle.

Sweet Plum Melomel

We serve this melomel with Asian foods. It is sweet, flavorful, and particularly nice with cashew chicken or sweet-and-sour pork.

YIELD: 1 GALLON (3.8 L)

4 pounds (1.8 kg) yellow plums, halved and pitted

4 pounds (1.8 kg) honey

1 teaspoon (5 g) acid blend

1 teaspoon (5 g) pectic enzyme

1 Campden tablet (optional)

1 package (5–7 g) Montrachet yeast

1 teaspoon (5 g) yeast nutrient

1½ cups (360 ml) orange juice, at room temperature

⅛ teaspoon (.625 g) grape tannin

1. Put the plum halves into a 2-gallon (7.6 L) plastic container. In a large enamel or stainless steel pot, boil the honey in water (1 part honey to 2 parts water — use the empty honey jar to measure the water) for 10 to 20 minutes, skimming off any foam that forms. (The foam will contain water impurities and beeswax residue.) Pour the honey mixture over the fruit and let cool.

2. Add the acid, pectic enzyme, and enough water to make 1 gallon (3.8 L). Add the Campden tablet, if desired, and let the mixture sit, well covered, for 24 hours.

3. In a jar, make a yeast starter culture by combining the yeast, yeast nutrient, and orange juice. Cover, shake vigorously, and let stand 1 to 3 hours, until bubbly; then add to the must.

4. Allow the mixture to ferment. We recommend racking after the most vigorous fermentation; siphon the wine into a 1-gallon (3.8 L) airlocked fermentation vessel. In about three months, rack into another airlocked container. In about six months, rack once again. Rack a final time right before bottling — about a year after fermentation started. Then bottle and cork the finished melomel, and store it in a cool cellar.

5. Age for at least six months before opening a bottle.

Raspberry Melomel

Raspberry melomel has an intense raspberry flavor — a little like sipping the essence of raspberries fresh from the garden. We particularly enjoy this wine in winter, when the snow is piled outside and summer's fresh fruit is an all-but-forgotten dream.

YIELD: 1 GALLON (3.8 L)

2 pounds (900 g) raspberries

3 pounds (1.4 kg) orange-blossom honey

1 teaspoon (5 g) acid blend

1 teaspoon (5 g) pectic enzyme

1 Campden tablet (optional)

1 package (5–7 g) champagne yeast

1 teaspoon (5 g) yeast nutrient

1½ cups (360 ml) orange juice, at room temperature

1. Crush the raspberries in a 2-gallon (7.6 L) plastic container. In a large enamel or stainless steel pot, boil the honey in water (1 part honey to 2 parts water — use the empty honey jar to measure the water) for 10 to 20 minutes, skimming off any foam that forms. (The foam will contain water impurities and beeswax residue.)

2. Pour the honey mixture over the raspberries. Add the acid, pectic enzyme, and enough water to make 1 gallon (3.8 L). Add the Campden tablet, if desired, and let the mixture sit, well covered, for 24 hours.

3. In a jar, make a yeast starter culture by combining the yeast, yeast nutrient, and orange juice. Cover, shake vigorously, and let stand 1 to 3 hours, until bubbly; then add to the must.

4. Allow the mixture to ferment. We recommend racking after the most vigorous fermentation; siphon the wine into a 1-gallon (3.8 L) airlocked fermentation vessel. In about three months, rack into another airlocked container. In about six months, rack once again. Rack a final time right before bottling — about a year after fermentation started. Then bottle and cork the finished melomel, and store it in a cool cellar.

5. Age for at least six months before opening a bottle.

Rose Hip Melomel

Rose hips are the fruit of the rosebush. They have a taste reminiscent of apples and are an excellent source of vitamin C. Rugosa roses provide the best hips. If you get your rose hips from more dandified roses, be careful of the source. Many of today's pampered hybrid teas are treated with chemicals.

YIELD: 1 GALLON (3.8 L)

4 pounds (1.8 kg) rose hips

3¼ pounds (1.5 kg) honey

Juice and zest of 1 large orange

1 teapoon (5 g) acid blend

1 teaspoon (5 g) pectic enzyme

1 Campden tablet (optional)

1 package (5–7 g) champagne yeast

1 teaspoon (5 g) yeast nutrient

1½ cups (360 ml) orange juice, at room temperature

⅛ teaspoon (.625 g) grape tannin

1. Place thoroughly washed rose hips into a 2-gallon (7.6 L) plastic container. In a large enamel or stainless steel pot, boil the honey in water (1 part honey to 2 parts water — use the empty honey jar to measure the water) for 10 to 20 minutes, skimming off any foam that forms. (The foam will contain water impurities and beeswax residue.)

2. Add the juice of the orange and the zest, and let the mixture cool. Pour the honey mixture over the rose hips. Add the acid, pectic enzyme, and enough water to make 1 gallon (3.8 L). Add the Campden tablet, if desired, and let the mixture sit, well covered, for four or five days.

3. In a jar, make a yeast starter culture by combining the yeast, yeast nutrient, and the 1½ cups (360 ml) orange juice. Cover, shake vigorously, and let stand 1 to 3 hours, until bubbly; then add to the must.

4. Add the tannin and allow the mixture to ferment. We recommend racking after the most vigorous fermentation; siphon the wine into a 1-gallon (3.8 L) airlocked fermentation vessel. In about three months, rack into another air-locked container. In about six months, rack once again. Rack a final time right before bottling — about a year after fermentation started. Then bottle and cork the finished melomel, and store it in a cool cellar.

5. Age for at least six months before opening a bottle.

Strawberry Melomel

This wine is so delicious that it's almost sinful! Clover honey seems to preserve the strawberry flavor best. The resulting wine is a sweet, delicate dessert melomel.

YIELD: 1 GALLON (3.8 L)

3 pounds (1.4 kg) strawberries

3 pounds (1.4 kg) clover honey

1 teaspoon (5 g) acid blend

1 teaspoon (5 g) pectic enzyme

1 Campden tablet (optional)

1 package (5–7 g) champagne yeast

1 teaspoon (5 g) yeast nutrient

1½ cups (360 ml) orange juice, at room temperature

1. Crush the strawberries in a 2-gallon (7.6 L) plastic container. In a large enamel or stainless steel pot, boil the honey in water (1 part honey to 2 parts water — use the empty honey jar to measure the water) for 10 to 20 minutes, skimming off any foam that forms. (The foam will contain water impurities and beeswax residue.)

2. Let the mixture cool, and then pour the honey mixture over the fruit. Add the acid, pectic enzyme, and enough water to make 1 gallon (3.8 L). Add the Campden tablet, if desired, and let the mixture sit, well covered, for 24 hours.

3. In a jar, make a yeast starter culture by combining the yeast, yeast nutrient, and orange juice. Cover, shake vigorously, and let stand 1 to 3 hours, until bubbly; then add to the must.

4. Allow the mixture to ferment. We recommend racking after the most vigorous fermentation; siphon the wine into a 1-gallon (3.8 L) airlocked fermentation vessel. In about three months, rack into another airlocked container. In about six months, rack once again. Rack a final time right before bottling — about a year after fermentation started. Then bottle and cork the finished melomel, and store it in a cool cellar.

5. Age for at least six months before opening a bottle.

Clove Metheglin

Like mint, clove is a fitting finish to a fine meal. It settles the stomach, aids diges-tion, and tastes wonderful. You'll want to keep some of this brew for cooking, too. We've used it for everything from soaking fruit cakes to flavoring frostings!

YIELD: 1 GALLON (3.8 L)

3 pounds (1.4 kg) orange-blossom honey

2 bags jasmine tea

1 tablespoon (15 g) whole cloves

1 teaspoon (5 g) acid blend

1 teaspoon (5 g) pectic enzyme

1 Campden tablet (optional)

1 package (5–7 g) Montrachet yeast

1 teaspoon (5 g) yeast nutrient

1½ cups (360 ml) orange juice, at room temperature

¼ teaspoon (1.25 g) grape tannin

1. In a large enamel or stainless steel pot, boil the honey in water (1 part honey to 2 parts water — use the empty honey jar to measure the water) for 10 to 20 minutes, skimming off any foam that forms. (The foam will contain water impurities and beeswax residue.)

2. Brew the tea by steeping the tea bags in 1 cup (240 ml) of boiling water for 5 minutes. Add the tea and cloves to the honey mixture and let cool. Transfer the mixture to a 2-gallon (7.6 L) plastic container. Add the acid, pectic enzyme, and enough water to make 1 gallon (3.8 L). Add the Campden tablet, if desired, and let the mixture sit, well covered, for 24 hours.

3. In a jar, make a yeast starter culture by combining the yeast, yeast nutrient, and orange juice. Cover, shake vigorously, and let stand 1 to 3 hours, until bubbly; then add to the must.

4. Add the tannin and allow the mixture to ferment. We recommend racking after the most vigorous fermentation; siphon the wine into a 1-gallon (3.8 L) airlocked fermentation vessel. In about three months, rack into another air-locked container. In about six months, rack once again. Rack a final time right before bottling — about a year after fermentation started. Then bottle and cork the finished metheglin, and store it in a cool cellar.

5. Age for at least six months before opening a bottle.

Fall Spice Metheglin

Inspired by a favorite liqueur, this white to golden wine has a rich honey flavor that is enhanced with spices.

YIELD: 1 GALLON (3.8 L)

1 vanilla bean

1 cinnamon stick

½ teaspoon (2.5 g) ground ginger

½ teaspoon (2.5 g) ground nutmeg

½ teaspoon (2.5 g) ground allspice

Juice of 1 large orange

2 pounds (900 g) clover honey

1 teaspoon (5 g) acid blend

1 teaspoon (5 g) pectic enzyme

1 Campden tablet (optional)

1 package (5–7 g) Montrachet yeast

1 teaspoon (5 g) yeast nutrient

1½ cups (360 ml) orange juice, at room temperature

¼ teaspoon (1.25 g) grape tannin

1. Put the spices and juice of 1 orange into a 2-gallon (7.6 L) plastic container. In a large enamel or stainless steel pot, boil the honey in water (1 part honey to 2 parts water — use the empty honey jar to measure the water) for 10 to 20 minutes, skimming off any foam that forms.

2. Pour the honey mixture over the spices and juice, and let cool. Add the acid, pectic enzyme, and enough water to make 1 gallon (3.8 L). Add the Campden tablet, if desired, and let the mixture sit, well covered, for 24 hours.

3. In a jar, make a yeast starter culture by combining the yeast, yeast nutrient, and the 1½ cups (360 ml) orange juice. Cover, shake vigorously, and let stand 1 to 3 hours, until bubbly; then add to the must.

4. Allow the mixture to ferment. We recommend racking after the most vigorous fermentation; siphon the wine into a 1-gallon (3.8 L) airlocked fermentation vessel. In about three months, rack into another airlocked container. In about six months, rack once again. Rack a final time before bottling — about a year after fermentation started. Then bottle and cork the finished metheglin, and store it in a cool cellar.

5. Age for at least six months before opening a bottle.

Ginger Metheglin

This metheglin makes a superb ginger-flavored marinade for chicken or duck. The ginger here is subtle, not overpowering. Or use this metheglin in a delicious wine cooler — a little like ginger ale, but with an adult flair. Just mix lime juice, ginger metheglin, and club soda or a lemon-lime soda and pour it over crushed ice.

YIELD: 1 GALLON (3.8 L)

3 ounces (85 g) ginger

1 cup (240 ml) white grape juice concentrate

Juice and zest of 1 orange

Juice and zest of 1 lemon

Juice and zest of 1 lime

3 pounds (1.4 kg) honey

1 teaspoon (5 g) pectic enzyme

1 Campden tablet (optional)

1 package (5–7 g) champagne yeast

1 teaspoon (5 g) yeast nutrient

1½ cups (360 ml) orange juice, at room temperature

1. Put the ginger, grape juice concentrate, juices, and zests into a 2-gallon (7.6 L) plastic container. In a large enamel or stainless steel pot, boil the honey in water (1 part honey to 2 parts water — use the empty honey jar to measure the water) for 10 to 20 minutes, skimming off any foam that forms. (The foam will contain water impurities and beeswax residue.)

2. Pour the honey mixture into the 2-gallon (7.6 L) container and let cool. Add the pectic enzyme and enough water to make 1 gallon (3.8 L). Add the Campden tablet, if desired, and let the mixture sit, well covered, for 24 hours.

3. In a jar, make a yeast starter culture by combining the yeast, yeast nutrient, and the 1½ cups (360 ml) orange juice. Cover, shake vigorously, and let stand 1 to 3 hours, until bubbly; then add to the must.

4. Allow the mixture to ferment. We recommend racking after the most vigorous fermentation; siphon the wine into a 1-gallon (3.8 L) airlocked fermentation vessel. In about three months, rack into another airlocked container. In about six months, rack once again. Rack a final time before bottling — about a year after fermentation started. Then bottle and cork the finished metheglin, and store it in a cool cellar.

5. Age for at least six months before opening a bottle.

Hoppin' Honey Metheglin

Our experiments with adding hops to honey wine turned out well. The hint of bitterness that hops impart seems to balance the sweetness of the honey to create a sophisticated honey wine.

YIELD: 1 GALLON (3.8 L)

Juice of 2 large oranges

2 teaspoons (10 g) fresh grated orange zest

2 ounces (60 g) golden raisins, chopped

1 ounce (30 g) loose Cascade hop leaves

3 whole cloves

3 pounds (1.4 kg) wildflower honey

1 teaspoon (5 g) acid blend

1 teaspoon (5 g) pectic enzyme

1 Campden tablet (optional)

1 package (5–7 g) Montrachet yeast

1 teaspoon (5 g) yeast nutrient

1½ cups (360 ml) orange juice, at room temperature

¼ teaspoon (1.25 g) grape tannin

1. Mix the juice from the oranges, the zest, raisins, hop leaves, and cloves in a 2-gallon (7.6 L) plastic container. In a large enamel or stainless steel pot, boil the honey in water (1 part honey to 2 parts water — use the empty honey jar to measure the water) for 10 to 20 minutes, skimming off any foam that forms.

2. Pour the honey mixture over the fruit and spices. Add the acid, pectic enzyme, and enough water to make 1 gallon (3.8 L). Add the Campden tablet, if desired, and let the mixture sit, well covered, for 24 hours.

3. In a jar, make a yeast starter culture by combining the yeast, yeast nutrient, and the 1½ cups (360 ml) orange juice. Cover, shake vigorously, and let stand 1 to 3 hours, until bubbly; then add to the must.

4. Add the tannin and allow the mixture to ferment. We recommend racking after the most vigorous fermentation; siphon the wine into a 1-gallon (3.8 L) airlocked fermentation vessel. In about three months, rack into another air-locked container. In about six months, rack once again. Rack a final time right before bottling — about a year after fermentation started. Then bottle and cork the finished metheglin, and store it in a cool cellar.

5. Age for at least six months before opening a bottle.

Lemon Thyme Metheglin

Lemon thyme metheglin adds a whole new dimension to poached salmon when it is added to the poaching liquids; we've also used lemon thyme metheglin as a component of a delectable dressing for a salmon salad.

YIELD: 1 GALLON (3.8 L)

1 lemon

1 cup (240 ml) fresh lemon thyme, loosely packed

3 ounces (85 g) tangerine juice concentrate

8 ounces (240 g) light raisins

3 pounds (1.4 kg) honey

1 teaspoon (5 g) acid blend

1 teaspoon (5 g) pectic enzyme

1 Campden tablet (optional)

1 package (5–7 g) wine yeast

1 teaspoon (5 g) yeast nutrient

1½ cups (360 ml) orange juice, at room temperature

1. Use a zester to remove the outer rind from the lemon, discarding the white inner rind. Slice the lemon and place it, with the zest, in a 2-gallon (7.6 L) plastic container. Add the lemon thyme, tangerine juice concentrate, and raisins to the container. In a large enamel or stainless steel pot, boil the honey in water (1 part honey to 2 parts water — use the empty honey jar to measure the water) for 10 to 20 minutes, skimming off any foam that forms.

2. Let cool, and then transfer the honey mixture to the container. Add the acid, pectic enzyme, and enough water to make 1 gallon (3.8 L). Add the Campden tablet, if desired, and let the mixture sit, well covered, for 24 hours.

3. In a jar, make a yeast starter culture by combining the yeast, yeast nutrient, and orange juice. Cover, shake vigorously, and let stand 1 to 3 hours, until bubbly; then add to the must.

4. Allow the mixture to ferment. We recommend racking after the most vigorous fermentation; siphon the wine into a 1-gallon (3.8 L) airlocked fermentation vessel. In about three months, rack into another airlocked container. In about six months, rack once again. Rack a final time right before bottling — about a year after fermentation started. Then bottle and cork the finished metheglin, and store it in a cool cellar.

5. Age for at least six months before opening a bottle.

Mandarin Metheglin

If you prefer a little less zip in your citrus-flavored wine, the combination of honey and mellow mandarins will make this one of your favorites.

YIELD: 1 GALLON (3.8 L)

1 cup (240 ml) canned mandarin oranges with juice

1 tablespoon (15 g) fresh diced ginger

2 star anise flowers

½ teaspoon (2.5 g) ground cloves

1 cinnamon stick

3 pounds (1.4 kg) orange-blossom honey

1 teaspoon (5 g) acid blend

1 teaspoon (5 g) pectic enzyme

1 Campden tablet (optional)

1 package (5–7 g) Montrachet yeast

1 teaspoon (5 g) yeast nutrient

1½ cups (360 ml) orange juice, at room temperature

¼ teaspoon (1.25 g) grape tannin

1. Put the mandarin oranges, ginger, anise flowers, cloves, and cinnamon into a 2-gallon (7.6 L) plastic container. In a large enamel or stainless steel pot, boil the honey in water (1 part honey to 2 parts water — use the empty honey jar to measure the water) for 10 to 20 minutes, skimming off any foam that forms. (The foam will contain water impurities and beeswax residue.)

2. Pour the honey mixture over the fruit and spices. Add the acid, pectic enzyme, and enough water to make 1 gallon (3.8 L). Add the Campden tablet, if desired, and let the mixture sit, well covered, for 24 hours.

3. In a jar, make a yeast starter culture by combining the yeast, yeast nutrient, and orange juice. Cover, shake vigorously, and let stand 1 to 3 hours, until bubbly; then add to the must.

4. Add the tannin and allow the mixture to ferment. We recommend racking after the most vigorous fermentation; siphon the wine into a 1-gallon (3.8 L) airlocked fermentation vessel. In about three months, rack into another air-locked container. In about six months, rack once again. Rack a final time right before bottling — about a year after fermentation started. Then bottle and cork the finished metheglin, and store it in a cool cellar.

5. Age for at least six months before opening a bottle.

Mint Metheglin

A little like a mild crème de menthe, this wine makes a fine after-dinner drink. Sip it slowly in a cordial glass or add it to hot tea for a grand finale to your meal.

YIELD: 1 GALLON (3.8 L)

½ cup (120 ml) freshly picked mint leaves, chopped

3 pounds (1.4 kg) clover honey

1 teaspoon (5 g) acid blend

1 teaspoon (5 g) pectic enzyme

1 Campden tablet (optional)

1 package (5–7 g) Montrachet yeast

1 teaspoon (5 g) yeast nutrient

1½ cups (360 ml) orange juice, at room temperature

¼ teaspoon (1.25 g) grape tannin

1. Place the mint in a 2-gallon (7.6 L) plastic container. In a large enamel or stainless steel pot, boil the honey in water (1 part honey to 2 parts water) for 10 to 20 minutes, skimming off any foam that forms.

2. Let cool, and then pour the honey mixture over the mint leaves. Add the acid, pectic enzyme, and enough water to make 1 gallon (3.8 L). Add the Campden tablet, if desired, and let the mixture sit, well covered, for 24 hours.

3. In a jar, make a yeast starter culture by combining the yeast, yeast nutrient, and orange juice. Cover, shake vigorously, and let stand 1 to 3 hours, until bubbly; then add to the must.

4. Add the tannin and allow the mixture to ferment. We recommend racking after the most vigorous fermentation; siphon the wine into a 1-gallon (3.8 L) airlocked fermentation vessel. In about three months, rack into another air-locked container. In about six months, rack once again. Rack a final time right before bottling — about a year after fermentation started. Then bottle and cork the finished metheglin, and store in a cool cellar.

5. Age for at least six months before opening a bottle.

VARIATIONS: Mint Medley Wines

Spearmint, applemint, pineapple mint — the varieties of mint all give you metheglins with distinctive flavors. Try substituting your favorite flavor for the peppermint.

Rocky Mountain Red Metheglin

When we spent a summer in the Colorado Rocky Mountains, we found that hummingbirds love Red Zinger tea. Once we tasted this metheglin, made with that tea, we knew why those little hummers enjoyed it so much!

YIELD: 1 GALLON (3.8 L)

3 pounds (1.4 kg) orange-blossom honey

1 cinnamon stick

⅛ teaspoon (.625 g) ground cloves

2 teaspoons (10 g) freshly grated orange zest

Juice of 2 large oranges

8 Red Zinger tea bags

1 teaspoon (5 g) acid blend

1 teaspoon (5 g) pectic enzyme

1 Campden tablet (optional)

1 package (5–7 g) Montrachet yeast

1 teaspoon (5 g) yeast nutrient

1½ cups (360 ml) orange juice, at room temperature

¼ teaspoon (1.25 g) grape tannin

1. In a large enamel or stainless steel pot, boil the honey in water (1 part honey to 2 parts water) for 10 to 20 minutes, skimming off any foam that forms. Add the cinnamon, cloves, zest, and the juice of the oranges. Let cool, and then transfer the honey mixture to a 2-gallon (7.6 L) plastic container. Steep the tea bags in 2 cups (480 ml) of boiling water. Pour the brewed tea into the container with the honey and spices. Add the acid, pectic enzyme, and enough water to make 1 gallon (3.8 L). Add the Campden tablet, if desired, and let the mixture sit, well covered, for 24 hours.

2. In a jar, make a yeast starter culture by combining the yeast, yeast nutrient, and the 1½ cups (360 ml) orange juice. Cover, shake vigorously, and let stand 1 to 3 hours, until bubbly; then add to the must.

3. Add the tannin and allow the mixture to ferment. Siphon the wine into a 1-gallon (3.8 L) airlocked fermentation vessel. In about three months, rack into another airlocked container. In about six months, rack once again. Rack a final time right before bottling — about a year after fermentation started. Then bottle and cork the finished metheglin, and store in a cool cellar.

4. Age for at least six months before opening a bottle.

Rose Petal Metheglin

This wine is reminiscent of the Egyptian delicacy rose water, and can be used in many Middle Eastern recipes that call for that ingredient. It's a perfect accompaniment for light desserts and nutty cheeses.

YIELD: 1 GALLON (3.8 L)

2 quarts (about 1 L) loosely packed rose petals

Juice and peel of 1 lemon

Juice and peel of 1 orange

¾ pound (340 g) white raisins, *or* 1 pint (480 ml) grape juice concentrate

2½ pounds (1.14 kg) honey

1 teaspoon (5 g) acid blend

1 teaspoon (5 g) pectic enzyme

1 Campden tablet (optional)

1 package (5–7 g) wine yeast

1 teaspoon (5 g) yeast nutrient

1½ cups (360 ml) orange juice, at room temperature

1. Wash the petals under cool water and place them into a 2-gallon (7.6 L) plastic container. Peel the lemon and orange; remove the white inner rind and discard. Slice the lemon and orange, and put the zest and slices into the container with the rose petals. Add the raisins (or grape juice concentrate, if you prefer).

2. In a large enamel or stainless steel pot, boil the honey in water (1 part honey to 2 parts water) for 10 to 20 minutes, skimming off any foam that forms. Pour the honey mixture over the fruit and petals and let cool. Add the acid, pectic enzyme, and enough water to make 1 gallon (3.8 L). Add the Campden tablet, if desired, and let the mixture sit, well covered, for 24 hours.

3. In a jar, make a yeast starter culture by combining the yeast, yeast nutrient, and the 1½ cups (360 ml) orange juice. Cover, shake vigorously, and let stand 1 to 3 hours, until bubbly; then add to the must.

4. Allow the mixture to ferment. Siphon the wine into a 1-gallon (3.8 L) airlocked fermentation vessel. In about three months, rack into another airlocked container. In about six months, rack once again. Rack a final time right before bottling — about a year after fermentation started. Then bottle and cork the finished mead, and store in a cool cellar.

5. Age for at least six months before opening a bottle.

Rosemary-Lavender Metheglin

This wine has a nice, subtle bouquet and a delightfully different flavor. It's great with leg of lamb or a hearty lamb stew.

YIELD: 1 GALLON (3.8 L)

½ cup (120 ml) fresh rosemary

¼ cup (60 ml) lavender flowers

2 teaspoons (10 g) lemon zest

⅛ teaspoon (.625 g) ground cardamom

2 teaspoons (10 g) dried hibiscus flowers

3 pounds (1.4 kg) orange-blossom honey

1 teaspoon (5 g) acid blend

1 teaspoon (5 g) pectic enzyme

1 Campden tablet (optional)

1 package (5–7 g) Montrachet yeast

1 teaspoon (5 g) yeast nutrient

1½ cups (360 ml) orange juice, at room temperature

¼ teaspoon (1.25 g) grape tannin

1. Put the rosemary, lavender, lemon zest, cardamom, and hibiscus into a 2-gallon (7.6 L) plastic container. In a large enamel or stainless steel pot, boil the honey in water (1 part honey to 2 parts water) for 10 to 20 minutes, skimming off any foam that forms. Let the mixture cool, and then transfer it to the 2-gallon container. Add the acid, pectic enzyme, and enough water to make 1 gallon (3.8 L). Add the Campden tablet, if desired, and let the mixture sit, well covered, for 24 hours.

2. In a jar, make a yeast starter culture by combining the yeast, yeast nutrient, and orange juice. Cover, shake vigorously, and let stand 1 to 3 hours, until bubbly; then add to the must.

3. Add the tannin and allow the mixture to ferment. We recommend racking after the most vigorous fermentation; siphon the wine into a 1-gallon (3.8 L) airlocked fermentation vessel. In about three months, rack into another airlocked container. In about six months, rack once again. Rack a final time right before bottling — about a year after fermentation started. Then bottle and cork the finished metheglin, and store in a cool cellar.

4. Age for at least six months before opening a bottle.

Rosemary-Tangerine Metheglin

Rosemary-tangerine liqueur was one of the most popular recipes in our book Cordials from Your Kitchen, *so we thought we'd try some of the same ingredients in a metheglin. The results were as good as we expected. If you would like to try a delightfully different metheglin, this one is an inspired choice.*

YIELD: 1 GALLON (3.8 L)

3 pounds (1.4 kg) orange-blossom honey

½ cup (120 ml) fresh rosemary leaves

2 tablespoons (30 g) tangerine zest

6 ounces (180 ml) tangerine juice concentrate

1 teaspoon (5 g) acid blend

1 teaspoon (5 g) pectic enzyme

1 Campden tablet (optional)

1 package (5–7 g) Montrachet yeast

1 teaspoon (5 g) yeast nutrient

1½ cups (360 ml) orange juice, at room temperature

¼ teaspoon (1.25 g) grape tannin

1. In a large enamel or stainless steel pot, boil the honey in water (1 part honey to 2 parts water — use the empty honey jar to measure the water) for 10 to 20 minutes, skimming off any foam that forms. (The foam will contain water impurities and beeswax residue.)

2. Put the rosemary, zest, and concentrate into a 2-gallon (7.6 L) plastic container, and pour in the honey mixture. Let the mixture cool. Add the acid, pectic enzyme, and enough water to make 1 gallon (3.8 L). Add the Campden tablet, if desired, and let the mixture sit, well covered, for 24 hours.

3. Make a yeast starter culture by combining the yeast, yeast nutrient, and orange juice. Cover, shake vigorously, and let stand 1 to 3 hours, until bubbly; then add to the must.

4. Add the tannin and allow the mixture to ferment. We recommend racking after the most vigorous fermentation; siphon the wine into a 1-gallon (3.8 L) airlocked fermentation vessel. In about three months, rack into another airlocked container. In about six months, rack once again. Rack a final time right before bottling — about a year after fermentation started. Then bottle and cork the finished metheglin, and store in a cool cellar.

5. Age for at least six months before opening a bottle.

Royal Metheglin

The herbs and spices in this mead make it a drink fit for a king — or a queen.

YIELD: 1 GALLON (3.8 L)

3 pounds (1.4 kg) commercial honey

1 tablespoon (15 g) fresh rosemary leaves

1 tablespoon (15 g) fresh thyme leaves

3 fresh sage leaves

3 bay leaves

1 teaspoon (5 g) dried hyssop

4 allspice berries

6 cloves

1 tablespoon (15 g) fresh ginger, chopped

1 tablespoon (15 g) orange zest

1 tablespoon (15 g) lemon zest

2 bags Earl Grey tea

1 teaspoon (5 g) acid blend

1 teaspoon (5 g) pectic enzyme

1 Campden tablet (optional)

1 package (5–7 g) Montrachet yeast

1 teaspoon (5 g) yeast nutrient

1½ cups (360 ml) orange juice, at room temperature

¼ teaspoon (1.25 g) grape tannin

1. In a large enamel or stainless steel pot, boil the honey in water (1 part honey to 2 parts water) for 10 to 20 minutes, skimming off any foam that forms. When the foam stops rising to the surface, add the herbs, spices, and zests.

2. Let the mixture cool, and then transfer it to a 2-gallon (7.6 L) plastic container. Steep the tea bags in 1 cup (240 ml) of boiling water for 5 minutes. Add the tea to the honey mixture, and then add the acid, pectic enzyme, and enough water to make 1 gallon (3.8 L). Add the Campden tablet, if desired, and let the mixture sit, well covered, for 24 hours.

3. In a jar, make a yeast starter culture by combining the yeast, yeast nutrient, and orange juice. Cover, shake vigorously, and let stand 1 to 3 hours, until bubbly; then add to the must.

4. Add the tannin and let ferment. Siphon the wine into a 1-gallon (3.8 L) airlocked fermentation vessel. In three months, rack into another airlocked container. In six months, rack again. Rack a final time before bottling — a year after fermentation started. Then bottle and cork the mead.

5. Age for at least six months in a cool cellar before opening a bottle.

Chapter Five

MAKING WINES FROM HERBS

Wines made with herbs and spices are often among the most complex and sophisticated beverages in your cellar, not because they are more difficult to make, but because the flavors encompass a whole range of sensations — from strong and assertive to soft and subtle. To make them even more complex, many draw their flavors from a blending of the herb or spice with a grape or a honey wine, either of which makes a fine base.

No wine will bear your signature more clearly than those made with herbs and spices as their major flavoring component. But before you begin to blend these highly individual wines, you do need some basic understanding of the role of the grape in this exciting alchemy.

USING GRAPES AS A BASE

For the winemaker, three main classes of grapes are important: labruscas, which include the Delaware, Catawba, and Concord; vinifera, which produce the fine wines of Europe, such as Cabernet Sauvignon, Sémillon, and Merlot; and the French hybrids, which are grown in various parts of the United States and include such varieties as Vignoles, blanc de noirs, and the Seyval Blanc. Making wine from this wide array of grapes can range in difficulty from very simple to quite complex.

Consistently great grape wines happen only when the vintner is blessed with a good crop and knows how to treat it correctly. There are some underlying principles, however, that can help you produce good and sometimes even great wines. The difference between a good wine and a great one is somewhat subjective. Once we get away from the notion that only wines praised by some expert somewhere can qualify, you may find that your homemade wines have an edge. After all, they are custom made to suit your taste.

Red Wines

Red wines are, generally speaking, created from a red or purple grape variety whose skins are crushed along with the grapes and left in the must during the first fermentation. It is the skin that gives color to the wine, and the skins are also the source of natural yeasts that make it possible to ferment grape juice into wine without the addition of commercial yeasts (although most winemakers prefer to add the yeast, so they're sure of what they'll be getting). This marriage of yeast and grape probably accounted for wine's discovery in the first place — undoubtedly by some country dweller whose chance use of the juice from spoiled grapes started today's winemaking tradition.

White Wines

If the skins of a purple or red grape are removed and not included in the first fermentation, the resulting wine will be white, regardless of the color of grape used. White Concord wines are fermented this way.

White grape varieties with white skins (what we commonly call green or golden grapes) produce white wines with or without the skins. White grapes with colored skins will produce pink wines if the skins are left on during the first fermentation.

White wines, then, differ from reds because they have been fermented without the skins or because they have white skins to begin with, and these skins do not impart color to the finished wine. Also, white wines usually get racked one additional time before they are fitted with a fermentation lock for the second fermentation. For that reason, their flavors are often fresher than those of red wines.

EXPERIMENTING WITH RECIPES

In this chapter, we'll give you some of the recipes we've tried and liked, but we also encourage you to try some of your own combinations. We begin with a basic recipe for herb or dried-flower-petal wine (page 138), a white wine. This recipe has only two variations. The first decision you will need to make is whether to use grapes or raisins. If you decide on raisins, use 1 pound (450 g) of light raisins and enough water to make 1 gallon (3.8 L). If you choose grapes, use the juice of 3½ to 4 pounds (1.6 to 1.8 kg) of grapes and enough water to make 1 gallon (3.8 L). (Either use white grapes or omit the skins to ensure that you will have a white wine base.) The second decision is which of the many herbs, flowers, and spices to use to flavor your wine. Any of the flowers and herbs listed in the chart below can be added in the amount of 2 ounces (60 g) per gallon (3.8 L) of wine, as long as they are *dried*. Later, as you gain more experience, you will probably vary the amount somewhat to suit your palate. If you use fresh herbs or petals, increase the amount to 1 to 4 pints (.5 to 2 L), depending on your taste and the strength of the herb or flower flavor.

HERBS FOR WHITE WINES

Agrimony	Dandelions
Bramble tips	Elderflowers
Burnet	Lemon balm
Coltsfoot	Rhubarb
Coltsfoot flowers	Rosemary
Cowslip flowers	Rose petals

Herbs for Red Wines

Cardamom seeds	Cloves
Cinnamon sticks	Ginger

Herbs for Honey Wines

(Meads)

Balm	Mace
Cardamom	Marjoram
Caraway seeds	Nutmeg
Chamomile	Orange peel
Cinnamon	Parsley roots
Cloves	Rose hips
Fennel roots	Rosemary
Ginger	Rose petals
Hyssop	Sweet basil
Lemon mint	Sweet woodruff
Lemon peel	Thyme

Herbs for Aperitif Wines

Anise seeds (to produce a Pernod flavor)

Globe artichoke (to produce an Italian Cymar flavor)

Dried-Flower-Petal Wine

A surprising number of delicious wines come from flower petals. This recipe is a general one, so you may use any of your favorite herbs or edible flowers.

YIELD: 1 GALLON (3.8 L)

- 2 ounces (60 g) dried herbs or flower petals
- 1 pound (450 g) minced sultanas or other white raisins
- 2 teaspoons (10 g) acid blend
- 1 teaspoon (5 g) grape tannin
- 1 Campden tablet (optional)
- 1 package (5–7 g) wine yeast
- 1 teaspoon (5 g) yeast nutrient
- 1 teaspoon (5 g) pectic enzyme
- 1½ cups (360 ml) orange juice, at room temperature
- 2¼ pounds (1 kg) sugar for dry wines *or* 2¾ pounds (1.25 kg) for sweet wines

1. Place the dried herbs or flower petals in an enamel or glass saucepan with 1 quart (about 1 L) of water. Bring to a boil, lower heat, and simmer for 20 minutes. Transfer to a 2-gallon (7.6 L) plastic container and add the raisins, acid blend, and tannin. When the mixture is cool, add a Campden tablet, if desired, and let the mixture sit, covered, for 24 hours.

2. In a jar, make a yeast starter culture by combining the wine yeast, yeast nutrient, pectic enzyme, and orange juice. Cover, shake vigorously, and let stand 1 to 3 hours, until bubbly; then add to the must.

3. Ferment the pulp, loosely covered, for three days. Strain out the solids, or rack the liquid into a 1-gallon (3.8 L) fermentation vessel that can be fitted with an airlock. Add the sugar, fit the airlock, and let the wine ferment to completion. When you're sure the fermentation has stopped, bottle, cork, and cellar the wine.

4. Wait at least six months before sampling.

CAUTION: Whenever you use flowers in wine or cooking, make sure that they come from edible plants. The lovely oleander bloom is deadly, as are the flowers of lily of the valley. If you aren't sure whether a flower is edible, don't use it.

Lemon Thyme Wine

As with many herbal wines, this one is a blend of sophisticated flavors. The raisins or grape juice concentrate (you may use red or white grape juice) will give the wine its vinous quality; the orange juice adds zip; the rhubarb imparts a hint of tartness; and the thyme adds a mysterious hint of herbs. This combination makes a nice finishing wine for a fine meal. The wine's color will depend on the color of the grape concentrate or raisins. Using dark concentrate makes a red wine; dark raisins make a caramel-colored wine; light raisins, a golden wine.

YIELD: 1 GALLON (3.8 L)

2¼ pounds (1 kg) rhubarb

1 pint (450 g) lemon thyme leaves

4 pounds (1.8 kg) raisins *or* ½ pint (240 ml) grape juice concentrate

1 Campden tablet (optional)

1 package (5–7 g) wine yeast

1 teaspoon (5 g) yeast nutrient

1 teaspoon (5 g) pectic enzyme

1½ cups (360 ml) orange juice, at room temperature

2¼ pounds (1 kg) sugar

1. Wash the rhubarb and cut it into ½-inch (2 cm) pieces. Chop the lemon thyme, and put both ingredients in a large glass or plastic container. Bring 3 quarts (2.8 L) of water to a boil, and pour it over the mixture. Add the raisins or grape juice concentrate and let the mixture sit, loosely covered, for two weeks, stirring occasionally. Add a Campden tablet, if desired, and let the mixture sit, loosely covered, for 24 hours.

2. In a jar, make a yeast starter culture by combining the wine yeast, yeast nutrient, pectic enzyme, and orange juice. Cover, shake vigorously, and let stand 1 to 3 hours, until bubbly; then add to the must.

3. Put the sugar in a 2-gallon (7.6 L) container, and strain or rack the mixture onto the sugar. Add enough water to make 1 gallon (3.8 L). Cover the container loosely and let ferment for about two more weeks. Rack the mixture into a 1-gallon (3.8 L) airlocked fermentation vessel, and let the wine ferment to completion. When you're sure that the wine is finished, bottle, cork, and cellar it.

4. Age in bottles for at least six months.

Parsley Wine

Parsley wine was a surprisingly good entry at one of the wine tastings we judged. Some of the varieties had obviously not aged long enough to mellow out the slightly "green" taste. Those with the proper finish, however, were crisp, slightly tart, and very pretty. They ranged from nearly white to light yellow.

YIELD: 1 GALLON (3.8 L)

3 pounds (1.4 kg) sugar

1 pound (450 g) fresh parsley

2 oranges

2 lemons

1 teaspoon (5 g) chopped gingerroot

1 Campden tablet (optional)

1 teaspoon (5 g) grape tannin

1 package (5–7 g) wine yeast

1 teaspoon (5 g) yeast nutrient

1½ cups (360 ml) orange juice, at room temperature

1 teaspoon (5 g) pectic enzyme

1. Put the sugar into a 2-gallon (7.6 L) plastic wastebasket or bucket. Run cold water over the parsley in a colander or strainer, and chop it coarsely. Then use a vegetable peeler or zester to grate the outer rind of the citrus fruits, avoiding the bitter, white inner rind. Simmer the parsley, orange and lemon zests, and ginger in 1 gallon (3.8 L) of water for 20 to 30 minutes. Strain the liquid into the container with the sugar. Let the mixture cool. Add a Campden tablet, if desired, and let the mixture sit, loosely covered, for 24 hours. Then add the tannin and enough water to make one gallon (3.8 L).

2. In a jar, make a yeast starter culture by combining the wine yeast, yeast nutrient, and orange juice. Cover, shake vigorously, and let stand 1 to 3 hours, until bubbly; then add to the must.

3. Add the pectic enzyme. Let the mixture ferment, loosely covered, for about ten days. Rack into a 1-gallon (3.8 L) airlocked fermentation vessel, and let the mixture ferment to completion, racking as needed for clarity. Keep the mixture in the airlocked container for six months (parsley wines need to be mature before you bottle them). Then bottle, cork and cellar the wine.

4. Wait several months before you sample the wine, so it has time to lose its "green" taste.

Sweet Parsley Wine

Parsley wine is crisp and fresh-tasting, not at all what you might expect from a wine that starts out green! The finished wine is light yellow to golden, and great for the digestion.

YIELD: 1 GALLON (3.8 L)

1 quart (about 1 L) fresh parsley

2 oranges

7 cups (about 1.7 kg) sugar

2 tablespoons (30 ml) lemon juice

3 cloves

1 Campden tablet (optional)

1 package (5–7 g) wine yeast

1 teaspoon (5 g) yeast nutrient

1½ cups (360 ml) orange juice, at room temperature

1 teaspoon (5 g) pectic enzyme

1. Wash the parsley. Remove just the outer peel of the oranges (a vegetable peeler or zester works well), avoiding the bitter, white inner rind. Squeeze the juice from the oranges and set it aside. In a large glass or enamel container, heat the parsley and orange rind with 3½ quarts (3.3 L) of water, and simmer for 30 minutes. Strain out the solids and discard. Pour the liquid into a 2-gallon (7.6 L) plastic wastebasket or bucket, add the sugar, and let cool. Add the juice from the oranges, the lemon juice, and the cloves. Add a Campden tablet, if desired, and let the mixture sit, covered, for 24 hours.

2. In a jar, make a yeast starter culture by combining the wine yeast, yeast nutrient, and the 1½ cups (360 ml) orange juice. Cover, shake vigorously, and let stand 1 to 3 hours, until bubbly; then add to the must.

3. Add the pectic enzyme. Let the mixture sit in a warm place, loosely covered, to ferment. After 11 days, strain the mixture into a 1-gallon (3.8 L) airlocked fermentation vessel. After an additional 12 days have passed, rack into another 1-gallon (3.8 L) airlocked container, and let the wine mature for one year. Bottle, cork, and cellar the wine.

4. Wait six months before sampling.

Sage Wine I

Although often used in the kitchen, a number of country winemakers find sage wine equally satisfying in the dining room as an aperitif.

YIELD: 1 GALLON (3.8 L)

4 quarts (3.8 L) fresh sage leaves

1 pound (450 g) golden raisins

2 limes

4 pounds (1.8 kg) sugar

1 Campden tablet (optional)

1 package (5–7 g) wine yeast

1 teaspoon (5 g) yeast nutrient

1½ cups (360 ml) orange juice, at room temperature

1 teaspoon (5 g) pectic enzyme

1. Grate the outer rind of the limes, avoiding the white inner rind, and squeeze out the lime juice. Put the sage leaves, raisins, lime juice, and zest into a 2-gallon (7.6 L) plastic wastebasket or bucket. Bring 1 quart (about 1 L) of water to a boil, and then pour it over the ingredients in the bucket. Let the mixture sit, loosely covered, for 2 or 3 hours. Boil half the sugar in 1 quart (about 1 L) of water for 2 minutes, add it to the mixture, and let cool. Add the Campden tablet, if desired, and let the mixture stand, well covered, for 24 hours.

2. In a jar, make a yeast starter culture by combining the wine yeast, yeast nutrient, and orange juice. Cover, shake vigorously, and let stand 1 to 3 hours, until bubbly; then add to the must.

3. Add the pectic enzyme, and allow the mixture to ferment, loosely covered, for 10 days, stirring daily. Rack the wine into a 1-gallon (3.8 L) airlocked fermentation vessel, discarding the solids. Boil the remaining sugar in 1 quart (about 1 L) of water, and then let cool. Add it to the fermentation vessel with enough water to make 1 gallon (3.8 L).

4. Allow the wine to ferment to completion, but taste it before you bottle. If the sage taste is too strong, dilute the wine with a little water, and add 3 to 4 ounces (85–120 g) more sugar per pint (480 ml) of wine. Then let it sit in the airlocked fermentation vessel for another month before you bottle, cork, and cellar the wine.

5. Wait at least six months before you sample.

Sage Wine II

A little sweet wheat taste and a hint of mint give this wine a surprisingly sophisticated blend of flavors. We like to serve it in cordial glasses before dessert.

YIELD: 1 GALLON (3.8 L)

2 lemons

3 ounces (85 g) dried sage

1 pound (450 g) light raisins

1 ounce (30 g) dried mint

1 pound (450 g) wheat berries

2½ pounds (1.14 kg) sugar

1 Campden tablet (optional)

1 package (5–7 g) wine yeast

1 teaspoon (5 g) yeast nutrient

1½ cups (360 ml) orange juice, at room temperature

1 teaspoon (5 g) pectic enzyme

1. Grate the outer rind of the lemons, avoiding the white inner rind, and squeeze out the lemon juice. Put the sage, raisins, mint, wheat berries, and the zest and juice of the lemons into a 2-gallon plastic container. Pour 1 quart (about 1 L) of boiling water over the mixture. Cover loosely and let stand for 2 to 3 hours. Boil half the sugar in 1 quart (about 1 L) of water for 2 minutes and add to the liquid. Add a Campden tablet, if desired, and let sit for 24 hours, well covered, before proceeding.

2. In a jar, make a yeast starter culture by combining the wine yeast, yeast nutrient, and orange juice. Cover, shake vigorously, and let stand 1 to 3 hours, until bubbly; then add to the must.

3. Add the pectic enzyme, and allow the mixture to ferment for 10 days, stirring daily. Boil the remaining sugar in 1 quart (about 1 L) of water, and then let cool. Pour the solution into a 1-gallon (3.8 L) airlocked fermentation vessel. Either rack or strain the sage mixture into the vessel, stirring to mix. Add enough water to make one gallon (3.8 L), if necessary.

4. Affix an airlock and allow the wine to ferment to completion. Then taste the wine. If the sage taste is too strong, dilute the wine with some water, and add 3 to 4 ounces (85–120 g) more sugar per pint (480 ml) of wine. Then let it sit in the airlocked fermentation vessel for another month before you bottle, cork, and cellar the wine.

5. Wait at least six months before you sample.

Chapter Six

MAKING WINE COOLERS & WINE PUNCHES

Nothing says "party" so effectively as luscious punches and wine coolers, but the search for really unusual punches is every host's headache. Something magic happens, though, when your party punch is unique, derived from wines no other cellar can match. You can have as much fun experimenting with the coolers and punches as we did for this chapter — there was never a shortage of people who volunteered to come to a tasting party!

Presentation is important for party punches. Look for creative ways to prepare your punches for maximum visual impact. Freeze whole berries into ice rings made from gelatin molds or bundt pans. Float fruit-laden skewers in the punch bowl. Make colorful garnishes from mint leaves. Party punches should tease the eye, tickle the fancy, and tantalize the taste buds of your guests.

Iced Tea Cooler

Iced tea takes on a whole new personality when you include it in this deliciously different cooler.

YIELD: SIXTEEN 6-OUNCE SERVINGS (2.85 L)

1 cup (240 ml) mead of your choice (pages 105–108)

6 cups (1.5 L) strong tea

6 ounces (180 ml) lemonade concentrate

12 ounces (360 ml) cold water

25 ounces (750 ml) Lemon Thyme Metheglin (page 126)

Sprigs of fresh mint to garnish

Mix all the ingredients (except the mint garnish) and chill. Serve over crushed ice with the garnish.

Strawberry Wine Punch

If you like strawberries, you will love this sweet blend.

YIELD: APPROXIMATELY FIFTEEN 6-OUNCE SERVINGS (2.67 L)

1 cup (240 ml) sugar

½ cup (120 ml) water

2 cups (480 ml) Strawberry Wine (page 69)

2 cups (480 ml) orange juice

½ cup (120 ml) lemon juice

1 cup (240 ml) fresh or frozen strawberries, crushed

1 quart (about 1 L) seltzer or club soda

Mix the sugar and water in a saucepan, and boil it to make a syrup. Cool. Combine the syrup with the strawberry wine, the juices, and the crushed strawberries. Chill. Just before serving, pour the mixture into a punch bowl and slowly add the club soda. Serve immediately.

Tropical Wine Punch

For an unforgettable luau or tropical pool party, serve this easy-to-make punch in a bowl surrounded with red canna blossoms and make it the centerpiece of your buffet table. It's also luscious served in coconut cups — just drill a couple of large holes in each coconut, drain the liquid, and fill with punch.

YIELD: TWENTY-FOUR 6-OUNCE SERVINGS (4.28 L)

46 ounces (1.4 L) Hawaiian Punch

¼ cup (60 g) sugar

½ cup (120 ml) brandy

2 bottles (2 L) seltzer, club soda, or lemon-lime soda

25 ounces (750 ml) Strawberry Wine (page 69) or Strawberry Melomel (page 121)

Orange slices and strawberries to garnish

Mix all the ingredients except the soda and garnishes; chill. When you're ready to serve the punch, add the soda. Garnish with orange slices and strawberry halves or slices.

Passionate Fruit Punch

This punch is perfect for hot summer days.

YIELD: SIXTY-FIVE 6-OUNCE SERVINGS (11.6 L)

25 ounces (750 ml) mead of your choice (pages 105–108)

28 ounces (840 ml) passion fruit juice

1 gallon (3.8 L) orange juice

3 quarts (2.8 L) pineapple juice (unsweetened)

¾ cup (180 ml) grenadine

2 cups (480 ml) Rose's lime juice

2 gallons (7.6 L) ginger ale

Mix all ingredients together, chill, and serve in a punch bowl.

Blackberry Sangria

You've never had sangria like this! Our guests love it at holiday get-togethers — and any holiday will do. But it really sparkles when served with a make-it-yourself assortment of Mexican foods.

YIELD: THIRTY-FIVE 6-OUNCE SERVINGS (6.2 L)

1 gallon (3.8 L) Sweet Port-Style Blackberry Wine (page 46)

1 quart (about 1 L) orange juice

1 cup (240 ml) lemon juice

½ cup (120 ml) brandy

½ cup (120 g) sugar (or to taste)

1 quart (about 1 L) seltzer

2 oranges, thinly sliced

1 lemon, thinly sliced

Mix and chill wine, juices, brandy, and sugar. When you are ready to serve, pour into a punch bowl, add the seltzer, and garnish with the thinly sliced oranges and lemons.

Shooting Mixture

Prepare Shooting Mixture ahead of time, and keep a bottle in your wine cellar or liquor cabinet. Mixed with club soda or a lemon-lime soft drink, it makes a deliciously different wine cooler. Since the alcohol content of this mixture is high, mix — and consume — with caution.

YIELD: FOURTY-FOUR 2-OUNCE SERVINGS (2.6 L)

3 pints (1.5 L) Cherry Wine (page 49) or Cherry Melomel (page 112)

1½ pints (720 ml) cherry brandy

1 pint (480 ml) cognac

Combine all of the ingredients, and serve. Shooting Mixture keeps well if it is stored in a cool, dark place.

Yule Glogg

We like to serve this glogg whenever guests trudge through the snow to visit. It's warm and spicy and filled with good homemade wine and cheer. But it's a traditional Christmas season drink, so be sure to have some Cherry Melomel on hand for the best glogg you've ever served.

YIELD: FOURTEEN 6-OUNCE SERVINGS (2.5 L)

Juice and peel of 1 orange
(in spirals or pieces)

Juice and peel of 1 lemon
(in spirals or pieces)

¾ cup (180 g) sugar

8 whole cloves

2 teaspoons (10 g) cinnamon

½ gallon (1.9 L) Cherry
Melomel (page 112)

1 cups (480 ml) brandy

1 cup (240 ml) Almond Wine
(page 72)

In a large pot, combine the first five ingredients and bring to a boil. After 5 minutes, remove from the heat and add the remaining ingredients. Reheat just to simmering and serve warm.

Orange Cup Spritzer

This recipe makes one serving of this lively orange drink.

YIELD: 12 OUNCES (360 ML)

4 ounces (120 ml) White Clover Wine (page 79) or Parsley
Wine (page 140)

4 ounces (120 ml) orange juice

½ ounce (15 ml) Cointreau or Grand Marnier

Seltzer or club soda

Combine the first three ingredients in a large collins glass with some cracked ice. Fill the glass with seltzer or club soda and stir gently.

Hot Cranapple Punch

This punch is great after a late autumn hayride, a wonderful finish to a winter skating party, and a deliciously different finale to your favorite comfort meal.

YIELD: SIXTEEN 6-OUNCE SERVINGS (2.85 L)

1 quart (about 1 L) cranberry juice

¾ cup (180 g) sugar

3 oranges, pierced with a fork

16 whole cloves

6 cinnamon sticks

1 teaspoon (5 g) ground allspice

50 ounces (1.5 L) Medium-Sweet Apple Wine (page 40)

2 cups (480 ml) rum

1 teaspoon (5 ml) bitters

Heat the cranberry juice, sugar, oranges, and spices to boiling. Reduce heat and simmer for about 5 minutes. Add the wine, rum, and bitters. Simmer until piping hot; serve immediately.

Poinsettia Spritzer

The pretty color and low alcohol content of this spritzer make it an ideal addition to your holiday get-togethers. Garnish each glass with a sprig of mint or a strawberry if desired.

YIELD: 8 OUNCES (240 ML)

3 ounces (90 ml) cranberry juice

½ ounce (15 ml) triple sec

3 ounces (90 ml) Strawberry Melomel (page 121)

Seltzer, club soda, or lemon-lime soda

Chill all the ingredients, including a large champagne glass. Mix the cranberry juice, triple sec, and strawberry melomel in the glass; fill with soda.

Ginger Wine Punch

This is a great wine to serve at parties. For added interest, present the wine in a bowl with an ice ring floating at the center.

YIELD: THIRTY 6-OUNCE SERVINGS (5.3 L)

1 pint (480 ml) apple cider

1 pint (480 ml) grapefruit juice

1 pint (480 ml) pineapple juice

Juice of 1 lemon

25 ounces (750 ml) Dry Apple Wine (page 39)

1 pint (480 ml) brandy or bourbon

50 ounces (1.5 L) Ginger Metheglin (page 124)

1 quart (about 1 L) ginger ale or club soda

Honey or maple syrup, to taste

1 apple

Chill all the ingredients. Blend everything (except apple) in a large punch bowl containing a molded ice ring or a large chunk of ice. Garnish with diced apple or very thin apple slices.

Basic Wine Cooler

We like to make this with Sweet Parsley Wine, but any white or golden wine is delicious served as a cooler. Honey wines bring unusual charm to even ordinary wine coolers — and don't forget those brilliant berry wines.

YIELD: 12 OUNCES (360 ML)

6 ounces (180 ml) white wine, such as Sweet Parsley Wine (page 141)

3 ounces (90 ml) lemonade

3 ounces (90 ml) Sprite or other lemon-lime soda

Chill all ingredients, pour into a glass, and mix with a swizzle stick. Add ice if desired.

Cranberry Sparkle Punch

Part of the appeal of a good wine punch is its appearance. This sparking, clear red punch not only looks pretty, but also tastes so good your guests may want seconds — or thirds — so be sure to make enough for refills.

YIELD: FOURTEEN 6-OUNCE SERVINGS (2.5 L)

1 pint (480 ml) cranberry juice

Juice of 1 grapefruit

25 ounces (750 ml) mead of your choice (pages 105–108), or to taste

Juice of ½ lime

1 cup (240 ml) gin

Sugar or honey, to taste

1 quart (about 1 L) club soda

Maraschino cherries and orange peel to garnish

Mix all ingredients (except the club soda and garnishes) in a punch bowl containing a molded ice ring or a large cake of ice. Just before serving, add the club soda. Garnish with cherries and orange peel.

Wine Collins Cooler

If you find commercial wine coolers too sweet for your taste, you are sure to enjoy this dry version of a berry cooler. If you prefer an even drier version, you can substitute seltzer or club soda for the lemon-lime soda.

YIELD: 8 OUNCES (240 ML)

4 ounces (120 ml) Blackberry Wine (page 45)

1 lime

Lemon-lime soda

Maraschino cherry

Pour wine and a squeeze of lime juice (and peel) into a large collins glass half-filled with cracked ice. Fill with lemon-lime soda; stir and garnish with a cherry.

Lafayette Punch

A touch of sweetness, a tingle of bubbles, and the fresh taste of oranges make this a favorite Independence Day drink.

YIELD: TWENTY 6-OUNCE SERVINGS (3.56 L)

6 oranges, thinly sliced

Confectioners' sugar

50 ounces (1.5 L) White Clover Wine (page 79), chilled

75 ounces (2.2 L) brut champagne, chilled

Cover the bottom of a punch bowl with orange slices, and lay down a heavy coating of confectioners' sugar. Pour half of the clover wine over the oranges, and let sit for two hours. Add a cake of ice, and pour in the remaining wine and champagne. Serve immediately.

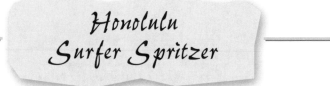

Honolulu Surfer Spritzer

If a cruise to Hawaii isn't in your budget, here's a taste of the islands that may make you want to hula the night away!

YIELD: 12 OUNCES (360 ML)

4 ounces (120 ml) pineapple juice

Juice of ½ lime

½ ounce (15 ml) Southern Comfort

3 ounces (90 ml) mead of your choice (pages 105–108)

Seltzer or club soda

Pineapple stick for garnish

Mix first four ingredients in a blender with cracked ice. Pour into a large collins glass and fill with seltzer or club soda. Stir and garnish with a pineapple stick.

Fuzzy Peach Fizz

A little like a fuzzy navel or a mimosa, this spritzer not only tastes wonderful, but delights the nose with its fresh peach aroma. Our guests think it's just, well, peachy.

YIELD: 12 OUNCES (360 ml)

3 ounces (90 ml) Peach Melomel (page 117)

3 ounces (90 ml) orange juice

3 ounces (90 ml) peach juice *or* fresh pureed peaches

3 ounces (90 ml) lemon-lime soda

Fresh sliced peaches and a sprig of fresh mint for garnish

Chill all the ingredients. In a tall glass, combine peach wine (more or less to taste), orange juice, peach juice or peach puree. Top off with the lemon-lime soda to achieve the fizz. Garnish with peach slices and a sprig of fresh mint.

Cranberry Shrub

If you add some pureed cranberries to this shrub, it makes a novel and delicious way to serve a traditional Thanksgiving favorite. Leave out the wine, add 7-Up, and even the little ones can enjoy the delicious taste and lively color.

YIELD: SIX 6-OUNCE SERVINGS (1 L)

2 cups (480 ml) any berry wine (see chapter 2)

1 pint (480 ml) cranberry juice cocktail

6 ounces (180 ml) pineapple juice concentrate

Orange slices for garnish

Combine the ingredients (except the orange slices), and pour the mixture over ice in a large pitcher. Stir to chill. Serve in clear glass punch cups garnished with an orange slice.

Bellini Royal Peach Punch

This delightful peach punch is a bit drier than the Fuzzy Peach Fizz on page 153, but the brut champagne adds a touch of tingle to the finished beverage. For a really dry punch, add only enough maraschino liqueur to give it a blush. For a sweeter punch, use enough liqueur to turn it a rich red.

YIELD: 8 OUNCES (240 ML)

3 ounces (90 ml) pureed ripe peaches

2 teaspoons (10 ml) lemon juice

Maraschino liqueur, to taste

3 ounces (90 ml) Peach Melomel (page 117)

Brut champagne or lemon-lime soda

Maraschino cherry and peach slice for garnish

Chill a large goblet or brandy snifter in the freezer for about an hour. Sprinkle the pureed peaches with lemon juice, and sweeten with the maraschino liqueur. Pour the puree into the chilled goblet, and cover with Peach Melomel. Add the champagne and stir. (For a milder punch, use lemon-lime soda in place of the champagne.) Garnish with a maraschino cherry and a peach slice.

Orange Cooler

For a Sunday morning brunch, this cooler is just the ticket. It's especially nice with salty breakfast meats, such as bacon, ham, or sausage.

YIELD: 12 OUNCES (360 ML)

3 ounces (90 ml) Pineapple-Orange Delight (page 57)

6 ounces (180 ml) orange juice

3 ounces (90 ml) lemon-lime soda

Chill all the ingredients. Pour the wine and orange juice into a chilled glass or over ice, and then add the soda.

Cherry Cola Cooler

If you sometimes feel like revisiting your younger, cherry Coke years, this cooler will take you back to the good old days — with a little more sophistication, but all of the memories. Cherry cola with punch!

YIELD: 12 OUNCES (360 ML)

6 ounces (180 ml) Cherry
Melomel (page 112)

6 ounces (180 ml) cola

Crushed ice

Orange slices

Maraschino cherry

Combine Cherry Melomel and cola in a glass. Serve over crushed ice, and garnish with an orange slice wrapped around a cherry on a toothpick.

Basil Cup

If sweet punches aren't high on your list of beverages, try this unusual punch. It's great served with nut bread and a salad.

YIELD: SIX 6-OUNCE SERVINGS (1 L)

1 cup (240 ml) sweet basil leaves

25 ounces (750 ml) mead of your
choice (pages 105–108)

Juice of 1 lemon

Thin lemon slices for garnish

Wash basil leaves, bruise slightly to release the flavor, and steep in the mead for 3 to 4 hours. Strain out the basil leaves, and pour the mead into a 1-gallon (3.8 L) punch bowl, pitcher, or individual glasses. Add a dash or two of lemon juice to taste. Garnish with thinly sliced lemon, either floating in the punch bowl or decorating the glasses.

Royal Raspberry Cooler

So delicious, it's almost dessert! This delightful punch tastes like fresh raspberries, and looks beautiful.

YIELD: TWENTY-TWO 6-OUNCE SERVINGS (3.9 L)

- 1 quart (about 1 L) raspberry sherbet or sorbet
- 25 ounces (750 ml) Sweet Red Raspberry Wine (page 63)
- 25 ounces (750 ml) Mandarin Metheglin (page 127)
- 1 cup (240 ml) orange juice
- 50 ounces (1.5 L) champagne *or* 25 ounces (750 ml) mead (pages 105–108) and 33 ounces (1 L) Sprite, chilled
- 1 cup (240 ml) fresh raspberries

Blend the first four ingredients in a punch bowl, and float an ice ring in it. Just before serving, pour in the chilled champagne (or mead and Sprite) and stir gently. Garnish with fresh raspberries.

Basic Wine Lemonade (Lemon Cooler)

This recipe works with almost any of your homemade wines, and each choice is an adventure — so experiment freely!

YIELD: 12 OUNCES (360 ML)

Juice of ½ lemon

Sugar, to taste

4 ounces (120 ml) homemade wine, any variety

8 ounces (240 ml) seltzer or club soda

Mix lemon juice, sugar, and wine in a large collins glass with cracked ice. Stir until the sugar is dissolved, and fill the glass with seltzer or club soda.

Tropical Punch

A take-off on the famous Bengal Lancers' rum punch, this tropical drink takes on added dimensions when you use your own blackberry wine as a flavoring component.

YIELD: TWELVE 6-OUNCE SERVINGS (2.1 L)

Juice of ½ lemon

½ cup (120 ml) orange juice

1 cup (240 ml) pineapple juice

½ cup (120 ml) lime juice

25 ounces (750 ml) Blackberry Wine (page 45)

3 ounces (90 ml) light rum (optional)

Sugar, to taste

25 ounces (750 ml) champagne

8 ounces (240 ml) seltzer or club soda

Orange and lime slices for garnish

Chill all of the ingredients. Combine juices, Blackberry Wine, rum, and sugar in a punch bowl. Add an ice ring or other molded ice form. Immediately before serving, add the champagne and seltzer or club soda gently, to preserve the bubbles. Garnish with thinly sliced oranges and limes.

Glossary of Winemaking Terms

Aerobic fermentation: Fermentation in the presence of air. Aerobic fermentation usually occurs at the beginning of the fermentation process, before the wine is transferred to an airlocked vessel. There, *anaerobic fermentation* will take place. Aerobic fermentation is usually the shorter, more intense fermentation.

After-dinner wines: Wines such as port, muscatel, and Malaga, often fortified but always sweet, that are consumed after a meal is completed.

Aging: Holding the wine in an airlocked vessel or bottle for six months to a number of years in order to allow the changes that occur after fermentation to make the wine mellower or more pleasing to drink.

Airlock: See *fermentation lock*.

Alcohol: Ethyl alcohol is the component in wine that acts as a preservative and an intoxicant. About half the weight of the sugar in the must will be converted to alcohol.

Anaerobic fermentation: This fermentation, in the absence of air, occurs in the fermentation vessel once an airlock has been affixed. Any air that was present in the bottle is quickly expelled through the airlock and replaced with carbon dioxide, a by-product of the fermentation process. Anaerobic fermentation is usually the long fermentation and the one in which almost all of the alcohol in wine is produced.

Antioxidant: A substance that prevents excess oxidation in wine — usually ascorbic acid — added to wine at the time it's bottled. A good test to see if you need to add ascorbic acid when you bottle your wine is to pour some wine in a glass and let it sit for 24 hours. If it turns brown, add ½ to 1 teaspoon (2.5–5 g) of powdered ascorbic acid to 1 gallon (3.8 L) of wine before bottling.

Aperitif: These dry, high-alcohol wines are served as an appetizer.

Atmosphere: Often used as a measure of how much pressure is created inside the bottle of a sparkling wine, like champagne. An atmosphere is about 14 pounds per square inch, and some champagnes are under six atmospheres of pressure. That's why you need special bottles for sparkling wines.

Autolysis: This term describes the process by which live yeast consumes the sediment in the bottom of a fermentation vessel. This process often gives wines a bad flavor, but it can be avoided by racking frequently so that your wine doesn't stay on the lees too long.

Bacteria: Microorganisms that may be found in wines or on equipment that is not sterilized. Different from yeasts, bacteria are often responsible for wine spoilage or for wine turning to vinegar. Yeasts that remain on unsterilized equipment and in unsterilized wine usually result in off-flavors, not outright spoilage. You can usually tell if your wine is spoiled by bacteria because it will develop an unpleasant (or vinegar) odor and a film will appear on top of a finished wine, indicating that oxidation has taken place.

Balance: A wine is said to be balanced when the components of the wine are in harmony with each other. These components include alcohol content, acidity, and residual sugar, as well as the flavoring agents of the wine.

Balling scale: A hydrometer scale that indicates the sugar content of the must in percentage by weight.

Body: The texture or fullness of a wine; the way it feels in your mouth. Body probably results from the alcohol and glycerin content — not the sweetness — of the wine.

Bouquet: A complex, rich smell that develops in wines as they age. (See *nose*.)

Campden tablet: Containing about 7 grains of potassium metabisulfate, a Campden tablet is dissolved in must or wine to release sulfur dioxide, which acts as a sterilant and antioxidant.

Cap: This term is used in two ways by winemakers. The first definition involves sealing the bottles against outside air once fermentation is complete. A machine is used to apply the caps. Most winemakers prefer corks, which can be applied with ease. The second use of the term "cap" refers to the somewhat firm layer of grapes or other fruit that rises to the surface of the must during the primary fermentation. Some recipes call for "punching a hole in the cap" to admit oxygen. The cap, as well as any sediment in the bottom of the fermentation vessel, is left behind at the first racking.

Capsule: The foil or plastic sleeve placed over a cork and the neck of a wine bottle to make a secure closure and to improve the appearance of the bottle.

Carbon dioxide: Fermenting yeast converts sugar in the must into carbon dioxide and alcohol in roughly equal proportions.

Chlorine bleach: A sterilant for cleaning bottles and equipment. Careful rinsing is essential. Chlorine bleach kills wine yeast and may affect taste if rinsing is not thorough.

Clarifying: The processes by which the suspended particles in a wine are removed — filtration, racking, and fining.

Clarity: The term used to describe the transparency or clearness of a wine. Wine should be clear and sparkling, not cloudy.

Color: A broad term used to describe the hue of the wine. Wines vary from nearly colorless white wines to deep burgundy reds with golden, pink, and all the shades of red in between. Clarity and color are part of the visual experience of enjoying wines.

Concentrate: A juice prepared commercially by removing water. In some cases, concentrates are mixtures of juices from different varieties of grapes or blends of fruit juices. Others are pure juices of one variety or kind of fruit. Be sure to read the list of ingredients on the label before using them in your wines. For concentrates packaged specifically for winemaking, the label will tell you how much wine results from that quantity of concentrate. With other concentrates, the label explains how to reconstitute the concentrate into juice. Usually water is added to juices in winemaking because normal-strength juices are too intensely flavored and too expensive to use. Avoid juices with added preservatives.

Dessert wines: Served with desserts, these wines are usually sweet and have a high alcohol content. Fortified wines (often served with dessert) have added alcohol to balance the alcohol with the sweetness. (See *fortification.*)

Dry: The term used by wine tasters to describe a wine with little residual sugar. A dry wine causes the slight puckering of the mouth that is one of the criteria for measuring sweetness. Wines may be brut (very dry), dry, semidry, semisweet, or sweet, depending on the amount of sugar left in the wine once the fermentation is complete. Most dry wines have about 1 percent residual sugar.

Energizer: Another name for *yeast nutrient,* usually containing phosphates plus vitamin B_1 (thiamine).

Enzymes: Organic compounds that make possible certain chemical reactions. In winemaking, enzymes are important in clarifying wine because they "digest" insoluble waxy pectins into soluble sugars.

Extraction: Describes the process or method by which the flavoring and nutrient components of a wine are obtained from the raw material — the fruits, vegetables, and so on. Methods of extraction include pressing with a wooden fruit press; using juice extractors, often called juicer-canners, which employ steam; boiling; soaking in either hot or cold water, and fermenting on the pulp, a process that lets the action of the first fermentation assist in removing the juices from fruits, vegetables or other raw material. Each method has its advantages, and winemakers generally adopt the method that fits their equipment and their preferences.

Fermentation: The process by which yeast turns sugar into alcohol and carbon dioxide.

Fermentation lock/trap: A device used to prevent air from entering the fermentation vessel while still allowing carbon dioxide to escape. Also called an airlock.

Filtration: The process of running wine through paper or other material to physically remove suspended debris from wine.

Fining: Describes the process of clarifying wine by removing the sediments and other agents that keep it from having a brilliant, sparkling appearance.

Fixed acids: Acids generally present in grapes and other fruits, such as malic, tartaric, citric, tannic, and phosphoric acids. They are "fixed" because they are nonvolatile.

Flocculation: Name given to the process of coalescence and settling of yeast cells into a firm deposit.

Fortification: The process of adding distilled spirits to a finished wine to increase its alcohol content, keeping qualities, or flavor.

Higher alcohols: Term given to alcohols such as methyl, amyl, and fusel oils, which may be present in minute, nonharmful amounts in some wines. If you distill wines, however, these higher alcohols become more concentrated and, consequently, more dangerous.

Hydrometer: A device that measures specific gravity in order to determine alcohol content or potential alcohol content of wine. Using a hydrometer allows the winemaker to adjust the amount of sugar in the must in order to have greater control of the sweetness or dryness of his wines. Hydrometers are available from many winemaking equipment suppliers and come with complete instructions.

Mead: Any wine whose primary energy source (sugar) and flavor are derived from honey. Honey wines need added yeast nutrients to complete the fermentation process, as these are not present in sufficient quantities in the honey itself.

Melomel: Any wine based on honey whose primary flavor is derived from fruit.

Metabisulfite: Sodium or potassium metabisulfite releases sulfur dioxide as a sterilant or antioxidant when it is added to must or wine.

Metheglin: Any wine based on honey whose primary flavor is derived from herbs or spices.

Must: The term used to describe wine in its very beginning stages, when there are large fruit particles, yeast, and juice present in the mixture.

Mycoderma: A spoilage organism that consumes alcohol and in the process impairs the flavor of the wine.

Nose: The aroma or bouquet of a wine; the smell that is released when the wine is swirled in a glass or warmed by the heat of the sipper's hand. A good "nose" is part of the enjoyment of wine drinking.

Palate: The term often used to describe the taste experience of a wine.

Pectic enzyme: An enzyme often added to the wine to digest the pectin in the solution. Pectins are the substances that cause jelling and are abundant in fruits such as apples — especially if they are slightly underripe. Winemakers use pectic enzyme to convert pectins to sugars because these waxy substances stay suspended in the wine and cause cloudiness.

Pectin: Substance present in some fruit, particularly underripe fruit, that is responsible for the jelling action in jams and jellies. In wines it stays suspended and causes cloudiness. It can be eliminated by using pectic enzyme.

pH: Describes the relative acidity of a solution. Because some acidity is desirable in wine, you want a pH below 7. A pH above 7 (neutral) indicates a basic solution.

Press: A device for forcing juice out of fruit pulp.

Primary fermentation: Also called the first fermentation or the rapid fermentation, it occurs in the presence of air. The most energetic of the fermentation processes, the primary fermentation quickly converts sugars to alcohol and carbon dioxide, causing a rapid drop in specific gravity in the solution. The length and ideal conditions for the primary fermentation depend on the kind of wine that's being made. (See *aerobic fermentation.*)

Proof: Describes the alcohol content of wines and spirits. It is equal to twice the percentage of alcohol in the solution; hence, a wine with 10 percent alcohol is a 20 proof wine.

Racking: The process of siphoning cleared wine from a fermentation vessel into a clean container, leaving the sediment behind. Racking gives wine its clarity as fruit solids, impurities, and yeast residue are eliminated.

Residual sugar: The amount of sugar left in the wine after the fermentation is complete. In wines, fermentation eventually stops when all the available sugar has been used up or when the concentration of alcohol reaches a point where further yeast growth is inhibited. Residual sugar that remains gives the wine its sweetness.

Rosé: A pink wine, usually made by allowing only part of the first fermentation to take place with the skins of red or purple grapes in the must. The skins are removed before they impart their full color to the wine.

Secondary fermentation: The slower, second fermentation that takes place in the absence of air, creating more alcohol as the yeast grows. (See *anaerobic fermentation.*)

Siphon: A device used to transfer fluids from one container to another, or the process of doing so. In winemaking, plastic or rubber tubing is often used in the racking process to transfer the cleared wine into a clean container. The siphoning process is often begun by putting one end of the tube into the fermentation vessel, just above the sediment, and sucking gently on the other end to get the flow started. Once the wine is flowing from the tube, the free end is placed in another container that is lower than the original container, and air pressure and gravity then take care of the rest. Siphoning is often called *racking* in winemaking circles.

Sparkling wines: Any wine that has been allowed to complete part of its fermentation in heavy bottles, without releasing the carbon dioxide produced by the fermentation process. Sparkling wines require special champagne bottles and careful handling because the contents are under pressure. Champagnes and spumantes are sparkling wines.

Specific gravity: Describes the density of a solution. When the wine has not yet begun the fermentation process, the specific gravity is high due to the suspended sugar particles in the must. As the wine ferments, the sugar is converted to alcohol and carbon dioxide and the specific gravity of the solution is lower. Specific gravity is measured with a *hydrometer.*

Spirits: High-alcohol-content beverages produced by distillations, such as brandy, rum, gin, whiskey, and vodka.

Stabilizer: A substance added to wine, usually ascorbic acid, that prevents oxidation.

Starter culture: A strongly fermenting yeast culture made from juice, yeast, and yeast nutrient. The culture is added to a larger volume of must to start the fermentation process.

Sterilants: Chemicals, such as Campden tablets, used to inhibit wild yeast and bacteria that may cause spoilage in wines. Also describes substances that perform the same function on equipment, such as an unscented household bleach.

Sterile: Describes equipment and solutions that are germ and yeast free — where no microbial growth exists. Winemakers sterilize their equipment to prevent wild yeasts and bacteria that might be present on their surfaces from contaminating the wine and causing spoilage or off-flavors. The wine itself is rendered sterile by using *Campden tablets*. After 24 hours, the wine is inoculated with the desirable yeast and fermentation begins.

Stuck fermentation: Describes a fermentation that stops without having converted all the available sugar to alcohol, usually due to some imbalance in the winemaking ingredients.

Sulfites: Sulfur residue left over from the chemical reaction that produces sulfur dioxide when a Campden tablet is added to wine. Usually harmless in the minute quantities in which it occurs in wine, but may cause an allergic reaction in some people.

Sulfur dioxide: A gas released by Campden tablets and other metabisulfites that sterilizes and prevents oxidation in must and wine. Harmless in recommended quantities, but may cause an allergic reaction in some people.

Sweet wine: Any wine that has enough residual sugar to give it a sweet taste — usually more than 1 percent. (See *dry*.)

Table wine: Any wine that is served with meals. It may cleanse the palate, stimulate the appetite, and provide subtle contrasts with the food flavors. Any wine that helps accomplish these things — in short, any wine whose flavor, bouquet, and consistency please you — may be served with food. Usually white wines are served with light-colored meat or fish; rosés with chicken or poultry dishes; and red wines with red meats, such as steak and roast beef, but these choices represent popular preferences only, not hard-and-fast rules.

Tannin: Astringent substance found in grape pips and stems, oak leaves, and tea. Needed in small quantities to improve the keeping quality of wines and to provide balance.

Topping up or topping off: The addition of wine to fermentation vessels from a reserve supply to keep the container full. The process reduces the possibility of oxidation. Also used for adding wine at the bottling stage to completely fill a bottle.

Yeast nutrient: The substances that yeasts must have in their "diet" so that they remain healthy and growing. Some wild wine recipes, especially some of the honey-based wines, are deficient in yeast nutrients, so these must be added in order for the yeast to continue to grow and produce alcohol from the sugars present in the must. Some winemakers compare yeast nutrients to "vitamin pills" for wine.

Resources

Retail shops selling home winemaking supplies can be a great source of information in addition to winemaking ingredients. To locate the closest home winemaking supply shop, look in your local Yellow Pages, which should have a listing under "Winemaking Supplies." Most retailers carrying home winemaking supplies also carry home-brewing supplies as well, so be sure to also look under "Brewing Supplies" and "Beer — Homebrewing Supplies".

In addition, you can access the Home Wine & Beer Trade Association's Web site at **www.hwbta.org** for more information about member stores that sell winemaking supplies located near you. On HWBTA's homepage, click Find A Shop in the menu on the left. You'll be taken to a page where you can search by business name, city, state, country, or zip.

You can also purchase winemaking equipment and supplies by mail-order catalog and on commercial Web sites. To locate on-line catalogs, type keywords such as "home winemaking supplies" into the search engine of your choice.

Index

Page references in *italics* indicate illustrations;
page references in **bold** indicate charts.

Other Storey Titles You Will Enjoy

Cellaring Wine, by Jeff Cox.
A sourcebook to create a system for selecting wines to age,
storing them properly, and drinking them when they are just right.
272 pages. Paper. ISBN 978-1-58017-474-9.

Cider, by Annie Proulx and Lew Nichols.
Thorough coverage of every step of cider making, from choosing
and planting the best apple varieties to making sweet and hard
ciders, sparkling cider blends, and cider-based foods.
224 pages. Paper. ISBN 978-1-58017-520-3.

From Vines to Wines, by Jeff Cox.
A complete home winemaking education in one
book — from planting vines to pulling the cork.
256 pages. Paper. ISBN 978-1-58017-105-2.

Fruits and Berries for the Home Garden, by Lewis Hill.
Instructions for the beginner and bushels of tips
for people who've been growing fruits for years.
280 pages. Paper. ISBN 978-0-88266-763-8.

The Home Winemaker's Companion, by Gene Spaziani and Ed Halloran.
A guide for all levels, starting with your first batch of kit wine
to mastering advanced techniques for making wine from fresh grapes.
272 pages. Paper. ISBN 978-1-58017-209-7.

Landscaping with Fruit, by Lee Reich.
A complete, accessible guide to luscious landscaping — from
alpine strawberry to lingonberry, mulberry to wintergreen.
192 pages. Paper. ISBN 978-1-60342-091-4.
Hardcover with jacket. ISBN 978-1-60342-096-9.

The Winemaker's Answer Book, by Alison Crowe.
A reassuring reference that offers proven solutions to every winemaking
mishap, written by *WineMaker* magazine's Wine Wizard.
384 pages. Flexibind. ISBN 978-1-58017-656-9.

These and other books from Storey Publishing are available
wherever quality books are sold or by calling 1-800-441-5700.
Visit us at *www.storey.com*.